FINDING MY PLACE

MAKING MY PARENTS' AMERICAN DREAM COME TRUE

ELIZABETH PIPKO

Post Hill
PRESS

A POST HILL PRESS BOOK
ISBN: 978-1-64293-559-2
ISBN (eBook): 978-1-64293-560-8

Finding My Place:
Making My Parents' American Dream Come True
© 2020 by Elizabeth Pipko
All Rights Reserved

Cover photo by Maria May

Post Hill Press
New York • Nashville
posthillpress.com

Published in the United States of America

For the dreamers, the weirdos, the misfits,
the rebels, the believers, and anyone who dares to be different.
This one's for you.

❖

A Note from the Author

Thanks for being here. That sounds strange, but I mean it. Thank you. Never in my life did I think I'd have the privilege to tell my story like this, nor did I think I'd have the privilege of having anyone curious enough to want to read it.

A part of me feels strange and even selfish, getting to tell my life story like this at only twenty-four years old. But I've lived through some things I could have never imagined for myself, and have seen and learned some things that I can only hope others will be able to learn just by hearing my stories, and not from personal experience. I've also had my own story told by so many out there, I thought that it was time to tell it myself.

If one person heeds my warnings, gets an ounce of inspiration, or even just smiles a little more from some of the things I have to say, then this was a success.

Table of Contents

1

People often ask my brother and me why we are as patriotic as we are. Others make fun of us for sounding "crazy" when we talk about how much we love the United States. Some laugh and tell us we don't know what we're talking about when we praise this amazing country. So I hope you can understand why I am as excited as I am to finally get to share my story and the story of my parents and grandparents, who risked it all so that we could be born in the greatest, most incredible and beautiful place of all, the United States of America. I'm going to start from the very beginning, because I think it's important to highlight just what it took in order to make sure that I was born an American.

Both sides of my family went through extreme hardships when emigrating from the Soviet Union to the United States. My mom left with her parents and sister when she was just ten years old, and my dad with his mother at twenty. They both left their lives behind completely, as well as friends and relatives whom both of them assumed they would never see again. They were escaping into a total unknown and with no real information about the country they were heading to. All they had were the hopes of one day living the American dream that they had all heard so much about.

With just ninety dollars per person, few possessions of their own, and no chance of ever returning, they were forced to set out on a journey that so many could only dream about. They were fleeing injustice, anti-Semitism, and a repressive political system many of us here in the United States cannot begin to understand. Both were leaving comfortable lives behind for a shot at a life in a country that to them was the embodiment of democracy and individual freedom. Like many before them, they risked everything they had and knew for an unpredictable future for themselves and generations to come. Both of my parents have incredible stories and backgrounds. And both deserve to have their stories told much more than I ever will.

Unlike my father's story, my mom's story revolves mostly around anti-Semitism. She and my grandparents always told me just how big of an impact anti-Semitism had on their lives back in the Soviet Union and stressed the importance of religious freedom as one of the greatest gifts many of us are too spoiled and ignorant to appreciate. My mother was often beaten as a child by neighborhood kids for being a Jew, with no other parents intervening in the beatings, which often left her scarred and bleeding. My grandmother was fired from her job as a popular news anchor after word spread that she was Jewish, with those in charge not wanting a Jew on television screens in the Soviet Union. My grandfather was a very well-known artist who was never allowed to paint what he wanted or to express himself if it involved his religion in any way. Both of my mom's parents came from very observant families, and though being a devout Jew was extremely difficult back in the Soviet Union, my grandfather made sure to never miss a religious service on a high holiday. He never brought my grandmother or great-grandmother along with him because of the risks of attending a synagogue, where people were often attacked or even arrested.

My grandfather had always wanted to escape. It was his status as a well-known artist, though, that made it practically impossible. My grandfather had often begged the government to allow him to travel to other countries in order to view the artwork of different artists around the world. However, he was never allowed to travel outside of the Soviet Union, as the government was concerned about the possibility of him not returning and embarrassing the Soviet system as others had. On one occasion, my grandparents were allowed to visit Finland, but had to leave my young aunt behind as "insurance" so the government could be confident that they would come back. My grandpa used to listen to his favorite station, Voice of America, on the radio, usually hiding in a bathroom or closet and making sure to cover the radio with blankets so no neighbors would hear the station he was listening to and report him.

In 1973, President Nixon traveled to the Soviet Union and made a deal with Leonid Brezhnev, then leader of the Soviet Union, which allowed for (to put it simply) the emigration of thousands of Jews in exchange for a certain number of tons of grain. And though the deal was purposely not publicized anywhere on the Soviet news channels, my grandfather heard about it on Voice of America and applied immediately. My grandparents knew that they would have only one opportunity to leave, so when my great-grandmother suffered a heart attack they thought could take her life, they had to make the difficult decision to stay or to leave her and other relatives behind. My grandparents, thirteen-year-old aunt, and ten-year-old mom left with ninety dollars per person, all they were allowed to take with them. Ironically, to give up their Soviet citizenship, they had to pay almost one thousand rubles per person to the government. So, my grandfather made sure to save up and borrow from friends and strangers in order to leave each member of his family staying behind with enough to make their escape if they ever could.

My father has a very different story. He did not leave the Soviet Union because of hardships. In fact, he often told me how well off he and his family members were in Estonia. Both of my father's parents were famous lawyers, with my grandfather being one of very few lawyers in the Soviet Union who had permission to represent clients in politically sensitive cases. Doing so often required access to different bodies in the government and sensitive information, and therefore, he ended up participating in many controversial cases in the Soviet Union, many of them even known in the West. He was involved in the case of the ship captain who was court-martialed and whose story became the basis for the book and movie *The Hunt for Red October*. He also represented family members of the Soviet Politburo, some of the most powerful people in the Soviet Union. At the same time, the government had set its sights on my grandmother because as a lawyer, she often advised Estonian dissidents. And for my grandfather, it would be extremely difficult to leave his established position behind, something he knew he would never get permission to do. This left my grandparents to decide whether to stay and face an oppressive regime or to say their goodbyes and let my grandmother try to flee with my dad.

With the incredibly difficult decision to escape having been made, their goodbyes said, and exit visas in hand, my grandmother and dad headed to the city of Brest to get on the first train of their journey. They had been stripped of their Soviet citizenship and therefore at this point were stateless, with no passports or identification papers. Once they arrived at the train station, they were told that the train standing on the tracks was the last one out, and that they would soon be closing the border due to the disruptions in Poland by the Solidarity movement. There were no more tickets being sold for the train, so the guards were simply taking people's exit visas and sending them back. This would have been a catastrophe for my dad and grandmother who would have never been able to rebuild their lives in the Soviet Union or attempt to leave again.

In that moment, my grandmother took my dad by the hand and walked over to the station master's office. She looked him dead in the eye and told him that she needed two tickets for the train that was standing on the tracks. At the same time, she took out a piece of jewelry that she had on her and handed it to him. She often says she knew that this was a matter of life and death for her and my dad. My dad always tells me that in that moment he thought they would be reported to police and sent straight to jail. Instead, the station master took the jewelry, opened his drawer, and handed my grandmother two tickets.

After coming to the United States, my father saved money for years so he could be able to travel to Europe and meet with my grandfather. My grandfather tried to get a travel visa to any foreign country that he could in order to meet with my dad, but with the government being what it was—and only again proving how vital it was to escape—my grandfather was denied with every attempt. He was left knowing he would never see his son again and suffered his third heart attack at fifty-seven and passed away.

My parents' and grandparents' stories are unfortunately not unique. So many people risked everything that they had in order to come to the United States of America. Many weren't as lucky as my family, either never getting to escape or perishing while on the way. There is no part of me that will ever allow their stories and sacrifices to be forgotten. No part of me can allow their sacrifices to be in vain or their legacies to not continue.

My parents' arrival in the United States wasn't easy, either. Arriving in a new land, with no friends or relatives to guide you, and being forced to find your way without even knowing the language of those around you is not easy. But my family did not crumble. Instead, they rose to the occasion and created a life from nothing, something you can *only* do in the United States of America. Both of my parents' families landed in New York, the city I have been lucky to call my home from birth.

My mom's mom went on to become a newscaster, working, very fittingly, for Radio Free Europe/Radio Liberty. My grandfather became the artist that he always dreamed of being, becoming known for many things, including his works that depicted Jewish life. He also became known for his portrayal of America and Americans, with this artwork displayed in museums around the world. My mom became a concert pianist, attending the renowned Juilliard School from the age of ten to twenty-four and has since performed all over the world, including at Carnegie Hall in New York City. My grandmother on my dad's side went on to teach at the New School for Social Research and New York University. She also wrote articles for various publications, including *The International Lawyer* and the ABA's *Law and National Security Intelligence Report*. And my dad became the first Estonian to attend two Ivy League schools—Columbia University and Yale Law School—and went on to practice law.

As you can see, I have a lot to live up to. But I also have a lot to prove to the world. Specifically, what it means to be an American and everything that can be achieved here, no matter where you come from. I grew up with my dad telling me stories about how he often had to decide between taking the subway home from school (which would cost one dollar) and having dinner that night. He once got jumped in the subway and was left badly beaten because he refused to give up his briefcase. Little did the muggers know that all he had in there was a toothbrush, some schoolwork, and an extra shirt—all his possessions at the time.

My family has lived the American dream. They turned ninety dollars into the life I know today, leaving me with an overwhelming feeling of guilt and responsibility. I understand what it meant to them to allow me to one day be born in the United

States and I not only have a legacy of desire, drive, and success to live up to, but a dream to live up to and make come true. I have to make sure that every single thing that my grandparents hoped for for our family becomes reality. I have to make sure that the sacrifices made long before I was even born were not made in vain. And I have to make sure that every single person around our country knows exactly what it means to have the privilege to be an American, something I am reminded of every single day.

2

I've been asked on many occasions where my strong faith in God comes from. Growing up attending a Jewish school and being taught all about how *Hashem* (the name for God in Hebrew) is not someone that you see but rather someone that you feel, I have spent my life constantly searching for those moments of feeling. I've experienced many of those moments and met many people who have given me that feeling. My family's escape to the United States and all that they were able to overcome is a huge sign of God for me. My brother is also one of them, as is my husband. They are both gifts from God I know I do not deserve. In my twenty-four years on this planet I have had many moments of feeling when it comes to Hashem. All of those moments have stuck with me over the years and helped tremendously at times of doubt, despite some being much bigger or smaller than others. But I have felt and known no reason as strong as the one that came into my life when I was just three weeks old. Because of this, I can confidently say that God not only exists, but knows exactly what

He is doing, a conclusion I am so grateful I was able to come to so early on in my life.

When my mom was pregnant with me and it came time to start looking for a babysitter, a family friend suggested a woman named Lida. With my dad traveling quite a bit for work and my mom being a touring concert pianist, it was pretty obvious that whatever babysitter they chose would end up playing quite a significant role in my life. They certainly could never have imagined just how significant that role would be at the time.

My parents are known to push things off until the last possible moment, something they did with finding me a babysitter and something they still do today. When I was three weeks old, my mom finally picked up the phone and called Lida. Luckily, she was not only available but desperate to find a job. She and her husband had just emigrated from Ukraine and were anxiously looking for work. To this day, I am convinced that God sent them to America as soon as my mom got pregnant with me, knowing that, one way or another, we were meant to be in each other's lives. After a few years, Lida soon became Lidunia, the nickname we still use for her today, and her husband, Iosif, became a very necessary addition to every visit we would have with her. To say that they became like grandparents would be an understatement. They were like the soulmates I never knew I needed, wanted, or deserved. Hands down, to this day, they are the best gift that God has ever brought into my life.

After my parents gave me the gift of a brother and Lidunia knew that she could no longer take care of two toddlers by herself (she was already in her sixties), she and Iosif became our dream team. They were with us every single day. In fact, I probably spent much more time with them than I did with my parents or any other relatives. Iosif taught me everything that I know. He spent thousands of hours with me from the age of three, teaching me math and always telling me that my abilities in the subject were unique. He finally taught me to ride a bike after we spent ten consecutive weekends practicing on a little hill in the Hamptons, with Iosif at seventy-five years old holding my hand and running down the hill with me, then dragging my bike back to the top and refusing to let me help, every single time. He picked me up from school and raced me home every single day because I asked him to, even after getting hit by a car, fracturing most of his limbs, and spending more than half a year in rehabilitation.

At one point, we started calling Lidunia and Iosif our fairy godparents. No other words can accurately describe what happens when two strangers come into your life and become more than family to you. Lidunia and Iosif had no reason to love me and no reason to treat me and my family like their own, but they did. They loved me like nobody else ever did, without any conditions of any kind and with the purest love in the entire world. Even after turning twelve and no longer needing a babysitter, I couldn't separate from them. Lidunia and Iosif became an extra set of grandparents and never left my side.

They say you don't know what you have until it's gone, and boy, is that the truth. In November of 2014, I got the worst phone call I'd ever received. Iosif had been diagnosed with stage four lung cancer and given only a few months to live. My entire world crashed down around me. You often worry about your parents and grandparents leaving you. But when God gives you the gift of a set of people whom you cannot live without, and a set of people you never knew you'd ever meet in the first place, it somehow never crosses your mind that one day they could be taken away. Somehow, maybe because I knew it would be too painful to bear, I never let my mind even consider the idea that Lidunia and Iosif wouldn't be by my side forever. It was a shock and a pain like none I had ever felt before. To this day, it was one of the worst nights of my life.

I prayed harder than ever before, hoping Hashem would hear my cries to save the one person that meant the world to me. I brought Iosif every herb and pill I could find and spent nights awake researching magical cures for his cancer, hoping that God would spare my favorite person from the pain he was going through and Lidunia, the best person to ever walk this earth, from the kind of pain that she would have to endure if we lost him. My brother and I spent weeks in the hospital with Lidunia and Iosif, begging doctors to do all they could to save our favorite person. At one point, his kidneys gave out and my brother and I sat by patiently, ready to give up a kidney in case a doctor told us that that was what he needed. I'm confident I wouldn't have hesitated for a second to give him a kidney if that was what he needed. In fact, I would have given him both.

The days flew by as if in a race. Thinking back, I wish I would have fought harder to spend every last second with him. But he was deteriorating quickly and didn't want us seeing what was happening to him, and I had yet to digest what was going on around me. On December 25, 2014, as I sat with my brother at a neighbor's house, I felt a pain in my chest as if a gust of wind had just flown through me. It was as if a hole had appeared suddenly in my heart. I looked over at my brother and had him call Lidunia, even though I already knew what the feeling meant. Iosif was gone.

Iosif and I had a bond more special than any I have ever seen. We were more than father and daughter, more than grandfather and granddaughter, and more than teacher and student. He was my absolute best friend in the entire world and the one person I knew would be there for me no matter what. He gave me the kind of feeling of love and protection that was somehow even stronger than what I felt from my parents. He called me his *kookalka*, meaning "doll" in Russian, and treated me exactly as such. He loved me for no reason at all except for the fact that God put us into each other's lives, for what reason we will never know.

When he passed away, my heart shattered. Five years later, I still wonder if it will ever feel whole again. He was the one thing I never realized could be gone one day and the one thing I still can't live without. He loved me unconditionally; I sometimes even question why God thought I deserved a love like that. Some days I wonder if I'll ever be loved like that again—not that anything could ever compare with what I shared with him, because nothing ever will.

I once read that the meaning of the name *Lida* is "sparkle," and that's exactly what she is. Lidunia has been the sparkle of my life since I was just three weeks old. She has been my mentor, my therapist, and my best friend since the moment I could speak, and I make sure to thank Hashem for bringing her and Iosif into my life every single day. Who could have thought that a couple living on the other side of the world could come to the United States of America and settle only a few miles away, just as my mother and father were having a baby who desperately needed them in her life? That's called the work of God, my friend.

Would I have survived without Lidunia and Iosif? Probably. Would I have turned out to be the same person? Absolutely not. They shaped me into the person that I am in every possible way. To this day, I need to speak to Lidunia to go over every decision I make or any problem that needs fixing. To this day, I hear Iosif's voice in my head telling me everything will be alright and not to cry, something I do way too often. He hated when I cried, and he'd be so angry with me for how hard I'm crying right now as I write this. Together, they gave me the gift of life. Not the gift of life that came from my parents, but the gift of a life filled with the kind of love that you only see or hear about in movies and fairy-tales. I'm probably going to keep crying, because the pain of living without my best friend is one I'll never get used to. But I'm also going to keep living and keep smiling with Lidunia by my side, exactly as Iosif would have wanted me to do.

3

Before I can even begin to talk about anything juicy, there is one last thing I need to bore you with: the reason that my life has panned out the way that it has, and the reason that the Elizabeth Pipko that you know today exists at all. It is all because of something extremely important to me, something that I love even more than I love most people in my life, in fact, maybe even more than I love life itself.

It was the spring of fourth grade. It was Passover break in school, and I went with my parents and brother to Florida on vacation. My parents had just purchased a small apartment in Boca Raton, and despite my brother and I seeing sand and the ocean for the first time in months, and my mom's insistence that we enjoy it, we had other plans. My brother and I are extremely close and until about thirteen or fourteen, I was basically able to convince him to get on board with any idea that I came up with. This time was no different. I had taken a few ice-skating lessons in Central Park and decided that was what I wanted to do while we were on this vacation. So as usual, I relied on my brother for backing as I bothered my parents during every free moment I could find to take me to an ice-skating rink. After a few days, everything became a lot less about me actually getting the chance to ice-skate and more about my stubborn nine-year-old self getting what she had been begging for. To this day I can't, for the life of me, even remember why I wanted to go skating in the first place.

After a fight with my mom (and her continued insistence that we stay at the apartment and go to the beach), my dad decided it was time to leave the house and take us to find an ice-skating rink. As crazy as it is to think about, his stubbornness during that fight is probably the reason that my life has gone the way that it has. After searching for a rink we had found online for about forty minutes, we finally arrived. Glacier Ice and Snow Arena was a small rink located in Pompano Beach. It was tiny and weirdly painted, certainly not eye-catching or resembling anything I had imagined in my head, but at least we had arrived.

As soon as we walked into the building, we were told we were too late to skate that day with just twenty minutes remaining in the general skating session. We decided to sit and watch what was going on out on the ice, though I was much more interested in the Pac-Man game I could see being played in the arcade in the back. Then, out of the corner of my eye, I saw a beautiful woman teaching a lesson. Her movements were like none I had ever seen before. My father, one of the toughest Russian parents you'll ever meet, turned to me and said, "If you ever want to learn to skate, it should be with her." I pretended to be disinterested in both this coach and skating altogether, but I'm sure the truth was written all over my face.

I had never wanted to be a figure skater. I never liked the pretty costumes, the idea of wearing makeup, or constantly being in the cold. I had never even wanted to be an athlete, and I certainly never thought figure skating would be the sport that caught my attention. However, in that moment, I felt a feeling of curiosity and ambition that my young self had never felt before. To me, it seemed as if my father was implying that I would not be able to handle the sport itself or a lesson with this incredible coach, and I was not going to let him be right. So, when we got home that night and my mom offered to pay for a half-hour lesson with this coach, I cautiously accepted.

Two days later, I let Nataliya yell at me for thirty minutes. I stood practically still for what felt like the entirety of the lesson as I was yelled at, and all my mistakes were pointed out in the most detailed and terrifying way. It was probably my favorite thirty minutes of my life. In that half hour, I felt things that I had never felt before. I was challenged at a level I had never been challenged before. I was motivated and supported by a coach in a way I had never experienced. I was inspired and moved by the art that Nataliya could create with her body on this frozen surface right in front of my eyes. I was humbled by the difficulty of a sport that I had never respected or admired (many in my family have always talked down on sports and athletes, which was all I had grown up listening to. More on that later). And I was excited for a future I had never before even considered for myself.

Those thirty minutes were all I needed; I knew what I was born to do. When I told my parents my new dream, they were amused, as I had expected, but more supportive than I had anticipated. They didn't look at me and say, "Sure, I'd love to throw away all the money I'm spending on your private Jewish school, advanced math classes, and violin lessons, and instead spend it on training for a sport that you're too late to start and have zero abilities in." Instead, my mom smiled at me in a way I had never seen her smile before, and in that moment, that was enough for me. My mom has always had a way of knowing exactly what I'm feeling or thinking in a specific moment; this time was no different. Was she ready in that moment to make all of the sacrifices that an athlete's parents usually have to make? Definitely not. But she seemed intrigued at the idea that I had fallen in love with a sport I had never previously shown an interest in, all in a matter of minutes. And it was nice to see somebody as intrigued and interested as I was in this new love I had just discovered. To be completely honest, I wasn't sure in that moment that I really was in love with figure skating.

I had spent thirty minutes in a lesson with an amazing coach and I wanted more, that was all I knew. I was a nine-year-old little girl whose emotions and excitement were all over the place, something I was very aware of. So I decided to let myself think for a little bit before I came to my parents with any grand ideas, probably because in the back of my mind I knew that my mother was going to let me pursue any dream I ever had, no matter the sacrifice, and I needed to be sure.

A few weeks later and back home in New York, I couldn't get skating out of my head. I was waiting for a good time to bring it up to my parents but hadn't found the right moment. One night at my grandparents' house (where I was spending the weekend), after waking up in the middle of the night and being unable to fall back asleep, I sat at the computer and searched the words "figure skating" on YouTube. Within a few minutes, I discovered Evgeni Plushenko, and I was hooked. I had never seen someone so impressive in my life. It was as if he was overflowing with talent with every step that he took. If I thought I was obsessed with figure skating before, it had reached a new level now. I knew that if I could ever do 5 percent of what he could do, I would feel accomplished. In that moment, every goal and every accomplishment I had ever had went completely out the window. Being the captain of the math team, playing the violin for six years, all of the painting I had done with my grandfather in the hopes of one day becoming an artist, all out the window. Nothing that I had accomplished up until that moment had any significance to me anymore. It was as if, in that moment, I learned the difference between a goal and a dream. I had never had a dream before; it was a feeling impossible to even try to put into words. Only today, fifteen years later, do I realize just how lucky I was to have even gotten the opportunity just to dream in the first place. That is something I certainly didn't understand at nine years old, and something many don't get to understand or experience in a lifetime.

It was my tenth birthday, and I had a plan. I knew that my parents couldn't say no to me on my birthday, so I decided to tell them then that I knew what I wanted to do. I had decided, after only a few hours on the ice, that I wanted to be an Olympic figure skater. I had never been surer of anything in my life. Even now, fifteen years later, I can look back and say that was the most confident I have ever been in any decision. It was as if I had found myself for the first time. This was a new version of myself that I didn't even know existed and one that I liked so much better than before. It was a version of myself that had no worries or concerns, only a passion and a dream making everything else in my life seem completely and totally irrelevant, which is just the way I liked it.

Two weeks later, we returned to Florida for summer break. My parents were set on us splitting all of our time between the beach and summer homework, but of course, again, I had other plans. We arrived back at Glacier Ice and Snow Arena, and somehow, this place that I had only known for half an hour already felt like home. Nataliya was still there, graceful and tough as ever, but this time, it was different. I knew that I had only six weeks in Florida to prove myself to this coach and to my parents, and nothing was going to stop me. I spent every single day at the gym and on the ice. If I wasn't on the ice or at the gym, I was watching old videos of Olympians and studying their movements. I had never been more committed to anything, and I wondered if the feeling would ever pass. Instead, it only got stronger by the day.

Around mid-summer, Nataliya introduced me to her husband, Sasha. They trained most of their skaters together, with her focusing on artistry and skating skills, and him focusing on technical elements. I wasn't advanced enough to start training with him, so instead I sat and watched him with his students every afternoon, consumed with jealousy. I watched girls half my age doing jumps and spins I couldn't believe were real while receiving coaching from this incredibly skilled man. All I wanted was to experience a few moments of that. Two weeks later, I got my shot. Someone had canceled a lesson, leaving Sasha with an available twenty minutes for me. Again, I humiliated myself for twenty minutes, attempting and failing at jumps that I had seen six-year-olds land with ease. But it didn't matter, I was one step closer to the Olympics, and that was good enough for me. Later that week, after my mom begged Sasha to find another twenty minutes for me, I overheard him telling her that he was going away for ten days and would try to see me when he got back.

Right away, I knew what I had to do. In those ten days, I spent every hour working on a waltz jump-loop. This was the combination jump that he had shown me in our first lesson, and despite most people not landing this kind of move in their first three weeks on the ice, I knew I had to prove myself to him. I watched videos on YouTube, I practiced the jump on the floor, and I fell on my butt a few hundred times a day. But eight days later, I landed it! Of course, I eagerly waited for Sasha to return in order to see what I could now do. And after showing it to him and following that up with, "See! I am going to go to the Olympics one day," he smiled at me in a moment that remains crystal clear in my head to this day. He barely knew me, and I had just mastered a skill I later found out was so elementary he probably should have laughed at me for even uttering the word "Olympics" at all. But I knew in that moment that a part of him believed in me, and I swore to myself that I was never going to let him down.

My parents are the best; it's as simple as that. When their ten-year-old daughter told them she wanted to go to the Olympics, they did what most normal parents would probably not do: they believed in me. Everybody told them how difficult of a sport it would be to pursue, especially financially, and they didn't bat an eye. Everybody told them how hard it would be for me, at ten years old, to begin a sport that most begin by four; they told me to ignore the warnings. Everybody told them how much effort and time it would take in order to get me proper training, so my mom uprooted her life and entire schedule and made it happen.

My parents began finding me coaches in New York. My dream was to move to Florida and train with Natalia and Sasha, but I knew I was lucky that my parents were even considering the type of effort and financial sacrifice it takes to invest in competitive figure skating, especially in New York City, so I kept my mouth shut and helped with everything I could. My parents were changing their entire lives for me, and I had to show them that I was appreciative and serious. Wollman Rink in Central Park, a rink owned by Donald Trump, was quite close to where we lived. The only time that I had available to practice was before school, so at four o'clock every morning, I made sure that I was awake and ready, by the door, waiting for my mom. My parents are the most supportive parents anyone could have, but with that comes a responsibility to live up to all the sacrifices that they make for me, something I was very aware of. The least I could do for my mom, who was waking up in the middle of the night to take me into the freezing temperatures in Central Park and paying for my practice time every day, was to be ready and waiting by the door for her every morning. I knew damn well what would happen to my dream if she ever found herself waiting for me to get ready. Four days a week my mom also picked me up after school and drove me over an hour away in order to get extra training from the coaches that Natalia and Sasha had recommended to me in Brooklyn, New York.

This was my life for almost two years. I trained two hours before school, attended school from eight until four, and then spent an hour getting to the rink, two hours training, and an hour to get home. Of course, my mom was always right there with me, helping me with homework, stuffing my face with bananas, covering me with a blanket as I dozed off on the car ride home, and anything else I could possibly need. We also spent every single school break, holiday, or long weekend in Florida so that I could skate with the coaches I loved. Basically, figure skating ruled the lives of my parents and nine-year-old brother, and they didn't complain once.

Two years later, it finally happened. My parents took my brother and me out of school, and we took off for Florida so that I could have the proper training that I needed. I had spent so many days too exhausted to skate properly at practice. Other days were spent trying to skate through the wind or hail at four in the morning at the outdoor rink in Central Park. I was living my dream every single day, but we all knew that it was no way to properly train for an Olympic dream. So, when my parents told me we were finally leaving for Florida, I was ecstatic.

Though I knew just how incredibly lucky I was to have the parents I had, it still came with many challenges. My parents had to live apart, with my dad traveling during the week for work (sometimes even to Europe) and then to Florida on weekends to see us. In our more than three years of living like this, he missed only one weekend. At the same time, my other family members were far from supportive. They didn't like the fact that my mom had picked up and moved our family for her daughter's "pipe dream," as they called it, and had zero problems reminding us of their feelings for months. I remember crying on my brother's shoulder as we heard my mom defending her decision to my aunt and grandmother while hiding in her closet, hoping I wouldn't hear the comments being said about me. That was one of the first times I was forced to learn the difficult lesson that sometimes blood doesn't mean everything, and to always remember that it is those who are related to you by blood that can have the strongest ability to destroy you because of how surprising their actions can be. My mom also decided to take my brother and I out of school and move us to virtual schooling. I had to catch up to the many kids who had started skating at a much younger age. In order to do that, I needed to spend over six hours a day on the ice—something I could not do if I was stuck in school all day. And despite what many people and even family members said about this kind of schooling, it turned out to be one of the best decisions we ever made. I was able to take honors classes, learn languages I never could have learned in school, and work at my own pace, including being able to skip ahead when I was ready. And though I'm proud of everything that I learned in Florida Virtual School, I could never compare to my genius brother who skipped four grades and was able to start taking college courses in the ninth grade. Take that, bullies.

The pressure of knowing that my dad was going to be working and traveling enough to affect his health, that my family was being torn apart, and that my parents were suffering financially over my decision to try to become a competitive athlete was a lot for me to handle. At just eleven years old, my entire family dynamic shifted simply because of a decision that I had made. Because of something that I felt in my gut and because of my mom and dad's unwavering support for my dream, everything was different. I also lost friendships I thought I would have forever due to this decision. My friends thought I was weird and used every opportunity they could find to make sure I knew that. Despite not feeling like I had changed in any way, suddenly after discovering skating, everything in my life that I thought I knew turned out to be wrong. All of the people I had loved and relied on for years seemed to disappear from my corner the moment I found something that made me happy just because it somehow also made me different, and they didn't like that. In a school that I had attended from the age of three—a school I once called my home away from home—where I was surrounded by friends I had known almost as long as

I had been alive, I spent my last few months eating lunch alone in the bathroom because nobody would sit with me.

I grew up with an extremely close family, with everyone (my parents' immediate families) living within two miles of each other and seeing each other at least once a week, something my eleven-year-old self never thought could change. Unfortunately, and as insane as it sounds, my family has never been the same since I made the decision to become an ice-skater. The family dynamic that I thought I knew had forever shattered in the blink of an eye. It was almost as if I had done something so unforgivable and awful that there was no turning back. I went through a lot of scenarios in my head, trying to understand what had gone wrong with both my family and my friends; however, nothing made any sense. I told people who I thought loved me and wanted the best for me that I had found something that made my heart happier than it had ever been before. Instead of being happy for me, they tried everything they could to stop me. It was then that I learned one of the most important, and most painful lessons we can ever learn in life. It's not often that you feel something so strong in your gut that you're sure it is meant to be. And in those moments, it's not just important to look around and see who is there for you, but who, in fact, is not.

4

My years on the ice were incredibly tough. Sometimes I look back and wonder how on earth my young self was able to handle all that I went through. The crippling anxiety alone would have been enough to stop most people, and yet somehow, I let it drive me to be better—something I wish I could figure out how to do today. There were days I would find myself standing in the bathroom vomiting over the toilet, still in my skates, knowing I had to be back on the ice in a matter of minutes. Other days, I remember feeling so sick I couldn't hold a cup of water in my hands because they were trembling so much. Before competitions, I wouldn't eat or sleep for weeks. I developed an anxiety disorder I'm not sure I would have developed if I had never started skating. And yet, at the same time, I also developed an incredible resilience to that disorder and to life.

Training at such an intense level is not something that the average kid deals with. It's something that is so rare and unique that there is actually no correct way to do it. What I mean by that is, anything goes. Literally anything. And if you met some of the coaches, skaters, or parents that I had to encounter when I was skating, you would understand what I mean. Young kids, as young as five or six years old, were taught to sabotage others. Parents bribed judges of easy basic skills competitions to make sure that their child ended up on top. The inappropriate interactions that were occurring all around me between skaters and coaches, or parents and coaches, are those you think only exist in movies. And yet, it was happening all around me, and everybody was acting as if it were completely normal.

I wonder sometimes how my parents were so confident in themselves and in the way that they raised me that they thought everything I was doing and encountering daily was a good idea. At one point, I was given what I was told were herbs that would stunt my growth, something every skater hopes for, as we're taught that our height could be what stands between us and greatness. At just five foot one, I remember worrying that my body was going to continue growing and keep me from the competitive career that I wanted. I remember sitting with my mom and telling her some of the truly disgusting things that certain male coaches had said to me, worried that she would take me out of skating forever. But she would just laugh and smile, totally unfazed. She would tell me stories of the abuse she dealt with from teachers at Juilliard, reminding me often that nothing I was going through was special and, more importantly, that it was not an excuse to fail or to quit. On one occasion, I checked my blades before getting on the ice for a competition only to find a tiny piece of tape on the bottom of one. A tiny piece of tape that could have seriously injured me, had I not noticed that it had been strategically placed there, as if right out of a sports thriller.

This was my life, and weirdly enough, I loved it. I loved feeling like everybody around me was out to get me, because it made me better. Every second that I wasn't training, I knew that my competitors were, and knowing how much they hated me at the same time made it all the more exciting. At twelve years old, I remember telling my dad during one of his weekend visits that a parent of one of my competitors had been caught recording me practicing. To me, it was the greatest compliment I could have ever received. For a girl who started so late and was laughed at by so many, having all these skaters, coaches, and parents worried about my progress was like heroin to me. As bad as it was supposed to make me feel, I only felt more invincible by the day. On one occasion, another parent sat with me before a competition and counted my calories as I ate my dinner, comparing it to his daughter's dinner as he loudly made comments about my weight. The world I had entered into was strange, to say the least, but it was thrilling and exhilarating and finally something that felt worth it. For the first time in my life, I felt like I was making a splash. More importantly, thirteen-year-old Elizabeth had just learned that she craved a life where she could make a splash, something I never would have known had I never stepped onto the ice.

I was constantly told growing up that sports were not for me. My aunt and uncle often made fun of athletes and those who respected them. I recall my family members laughing at my brother and me when we became big fans of basketball. Somehow there was never a missed opportunity for somebody in my family to tell us that we were silly and stupid for appreciating certain things in life. It was as if us being their idea of "proper" was more important than anything else in the world (even the things that could make us happy). And here I was, doing something because I chose to do it, something I knew people didn't understand or like, and I was succeeding. It was invigorating. I taped a quote by Oscar Wilde above my bed: "The only thing worse than being talked about, is not being talked about." Next to that, I had a printout of the Olympic rings staring down at me as I went to sleep every night. Together, that was all I needed.

Despite everything I went through as a young athlete, nothing ever surprised me. Maybe it was because of my parents' experiences in the world, their involvement in every aspect of my athletic career, and how they made sure I was always supported. Or maybe it was because of my overwhelming excitement for everything that I was getting to be a part of that I never noticed all the issues I was facing along the way. Whatever it was, I always felt as though there was nothing that could ever hold me back. I genuinely felt as though I was going to go to the Olympics. I probably would have put money on it, if I had had any money to put down. That was during a time in my life, one that we all go through, when we think that everybody gets what they deserve. Little did I know that that was not the case at all.

I really thought I was going to make it. I knew how lucky I was to have parents who could financially support my training, something many skaters do not have. I believed in the talent that everyone around me maintained that I possessed, and I knew that I would never, ever let anybody work harder than me. I was convinced that the person who worked the hardest deserved to win. And I was confident that God would make sure that exactly that would happen. But, as we're often told, "man makes plans and God laughs." If I had only known just how much God was probably laughing as I lay in bed every night with my eyes closed, dreaming about stepping onto the top of the podium at the 2014 Winter Olympic Games.

Now that I look back on those days, there must not have been a time that God was laughing at me harder than whenever I was lying on an X-ray table, which happened over one hundred times, being told what I had injured, and planning my return. My coaches, who had been involved in figure skating for their entire lives, were convinced that I had broken some kind of record. My neighbors laughed at the fact that they saw me on crutches more often than they saw me without them. It seems like every skating-related memory that I have revolves around an injury in some way, either fighting through one, recovering from one, or suffering one.

I broke multiple toes. I broke my foot, twice. I cracked my femur. I took a skate to the head (which left me with no eyebrow for half a year, a pretty graphic scar, and some solid nerve damage). I suffered two concussions. My tailbone has been fractured three times. And I completely destroyed my ankle. Nothing much, right? Somehow, after each injury—and sometimes even during—I felt unstoppable. My little teenage self was quite tough, the kind of tough I fear that I lost a long time ago.

There were days where I would pop a few Tylenols and skate through the worst pain in the world, somehow only feeling stronger despite whatever part of me was broken. In fact, I was just twelve years old when I cracked my femur completely from my knee to my hip, only to continue to skate on it every single day for three months. I even competed with that cracked femur and won three medals, performing better than I ever had before. At thirteen, my parents sent me to a two-week training camp that my coaches insisted I take part in. The camp consisted of workouts that would last up to ten hours on certain days, two half-marathon runs, and a daily meal limitation of six hundred calories. And as if the program wasn't brutal enough, I found myself stuck in the middle of that two-week training camp with a broken left foot. But despite the tears, which didn't stop for the remainder of the time I spent there, I completed the camp with my head held high. From the age of twelve to fifteen, I spent all four consecutive birthdays in a boot, brace, or cast with a different injury. What felt like a terrible running joke at the time has now become my favorite memory. Looking back, even as I write this, I envy myself. As sad as this sounds, I was so damn tough— emphasis on "was." I wish I knew where that came from, and I wish I could find some of it right now. No matter how literally broken I was back then, I was unstoppable, learning at an age too young to fully appreciate or understand that a broken mental state is much more dangerous than a physical one.

Eventually though, as they say, all good things must come to an end. And boy, did I learn that the hard way. One afternoon, on my second trip to the rink that day, I was trying to show off my abilities during an off-ice class, where we practice jumps on the floor. We were doing double axels—a jump where you take off from your left foot, rotate two and a half times in the air and land backward on your right foot. This was a jump I had done thousands of times, both on and off the ice, and yet, this was the jump that was about to change my life. I landed on the side of my right foot. I don't know if the floor was wet or if I was simply unfocused, all I remember was hearing a pop and feeling as though my entire foot was about to give out right under me. I walked over to the bench and took a seat, completely unaware of what I had just done. I thought to myself, "You just rolled your ankle. Wait three minutes and go do it again." But I couldn't. My ankle was a shade of blue and green that I had never seen before. The swelling and discoloration were so instant, I knew I had done something terrible to myself. It looked like I had taken a few magic markers and just went to town, and it felt as though someone had dropped a piano onto my foot.

The hospital wrapped my foot and told me nothing, scheduling an MRI for the following day. They told me that my X-rays did not look good, something I had heard many times before, which kept me more optimistic than they should have allowed me to be. I was convinced I would be competing again in a few weeks and went to sleep planning my comeback, something I had grown used to doing.

To put it lightly, the test results were not good. The doctor who originally saw me seemed less sympathetic than anyone I had met before. He began listing off everything that I had done to myself. I had bruised or cracked practically every bone in my foot, tore two ligaments and three tendons, and had a significant tear in my Achilles tendon. This doctor was unaware of my athletic aspirations and simply told me to enjoy the next four months of "relaxation" I was about to spend in my cast. My parents visited a family friend of ours, who was also a physician, to get another opinion. He looked them right in the eyes and said, "I think it's safe to say she's never skating again." After that, I let about five more doctors tell me the same thing before I could no longer take hearing those words.

I very clearly remember the first night I laid in my bed after realizing my dream was dead. I bawled my eyes out as my mother held me, just trying to get me to calm down so I could take a breath. I had never felt so sick in my life. My dream was gone, and it felt as though it had taken all of me with it. Imagine getting punched in the gut at the same time you find out you're never going to see your best friend again—that's the best way I can explain the feeling. It was a heartbreak and a pain I never knew existed.

All of a sudden, everything was over. We began to pack up our things, getting ready to move back to New York. There was no point in living in Florida and keeping our family separated anymore, and I couldn't blame my parents for wanting to get everything back to normal as quickly as possible. Within a few weeks, the life I knew was gone. I was back in New York City, no family or friends around me, continuing my studies online, sitting in a wheelchair, more broken than I ever thought I would be. When you spend your days doing death-defying tricks, and in the blink of an eye you're not only strapped into a cast but told that you'll never get to do those tricks again, it can take a pretty serious toll on you. Not only was the life I knew taken away from me, but it had taken who I was with it. I had only just discovered myself—my true self. And when I lost skating, I lost everything I had built over the past few years as well. All of my joy and confidence went right out the door with my ankle. Even now as I write this, ten years later, I'm not sure if I ever really got any of it back.

I had just learned why God had put me on this earth—at least that's what it felt like—and then, in the blink of an eye, that sense of purpose was taken away. I didn't want to go on. Within a few weeks, I was put on prescription medication just to try to function as a normal teenager. During that time, I also developed my worst habit to this day: I began to seriously harm myself. I couldn't forgive myself. No matter how hard I tried, I could not forgive myself for losing focus for that split second and letting gravity and a slippery floor ruin my entire life. Skating was all I had ever known. It was the only thing that gave me a feeling of purpose, the only thing that made everything worth it, and now it was gone and I was more alone than ever. I hated myself. I hated myself so damn much. So, I took to hurting myself as a way to cope with my anger. There were days where I tried other things. Some days, I would throw my trophies and medals at the walls while sobbing uncontrollably. Other days, I cut pieces of my hair off or simply starved myself as punishment. I didn't know what to do or how to go on. My dream had shattered into a million pieces, taking my heart and soul with it. I didn't think I could go on, nor did I see any reason to.

5

With losing your dream comes a lot of responsibilities, many that I wish I had paid attention to when I lost mine. When it came time to show my parents that I understood their sacrifices and the responsibility that fell on my shoulders when we moved to Florida, I never failed to do that. I made sure that every decision I made and every action I took made their sacrifices worth it. I made sure that they knew that I had understood, even at my young age, all that I owed them. However, when I lost my dream, all of that went completely down the drain.

I was heartbroken. I had never experienced such sadness before. It was the kind of sad I genuinely didn't even know existed. I didn't want to live, plain and simple. And unfortunately, I began living the kind of life that comes with not wanting to live one in the first place. Harming myself by using sharp objects to tear apart my skin only helped for so long. Eventually, the scars I would leave on my arms and legs stopped hurting, and I knew I needed more. Even the hair straightener that I would use to burn parts of my arm eventually began to bore me. My life consisted of my online studies, harming myself, crying, and sleeping—not exactly the teenage life everyone dreams about, but the one I got.

I remember desperately trying to put my emotions into words to explain how I was feeling to my parents. I refused to see a therapist, but knew I needed to at least try to speak with someone. And although I was given a lot of medication in hopes that it would be able to calm me down to a point where I could handle my emotions, I don't think I ever felt that it worked. And if it did, I'm pretty scared to imagine what I could have been like without it. I remember sitting in the bathroom early one morning at about four o'clock. I had just spent an hour crying and was desperate to put my emotions into words, if not to a person, at least to a pen and paper. This was the poem I wrote that night, and the first poem I ever wrote.

What's it like to lose a dream?
I'm a dreamer, trust me I would know,
Let me tell you how it goes.

First you lose the will to achieve,
Then you lose the hope to succeed,
Eventually you lose the will to breathe.

You are suddenly consumed by an overbearing depression,
Which eventually turns into hate and aggression.

Hate for everyone else in the world,
Every person, every animal, every boy, and every girl.

And just when you think this is as bad as it will get,
Something happens which you will never forget.

Suddenly the only person you hate is you,
And there is nothing you can say, and nothing you can do.

Nothing that could cause the hate to go away,
Instead it gets stronger every day.
And suddenly, you are left alone,

To a point where you can't feel comfort in your very own home.
When looking in the mirror causes disgust,
Because you've lost all belief in yourself, all the hope and
all the trust.

And when just living as yourself causes despair,
You lose the will to try and get air.
For your life is no longer a beautiful song,

And your only last wish is to be gone.

Is it impeccably written? No. Does it get the point across...
definitely. I remember bringing it to my mom and telling her
this was the most she would get out of me for a long time. Unfortunately, I think these few lines told her everything she needed
to know.

Although I was convinced that I was correct in giving up my entire life for figure skating, those around me were not. My family members once tried to convince me that by keeping myself from a "normal" life of friends and boys, I would end up miserable and lonely. And instead, it was losing my dream that left me that way. But upon realizing how much I had given up and replaying their words over and over in my mind, I began to realize that I now had access to the normal life of a teenager in one of the coolest cities in the world, and there was nothing at all to keep me from the bad decisions I used to judge others for making.

All of the things I thought I didn't want or need were now available to me, and though a part of me was convinced it was a world I wanted nothing to do with, another part of me was filled with curiosity. Everyone I grew up with was living a life that others around the world could only dream about. They were teenagers in New York City, living out the kinds of experiences I had ironically only ever watched on television. I had spent the last four years of my life locked in a freezing box, with no interactions with the opposite sex, living a life consumed by blood, sweat, and tears. I was convinced that my life was over anyway, so what on earth did I possibly have left to lose?

I began attempting to "live." Everything that those around me were doing, I decided to try. Luckily, by "everything" I don't, in fact, mean "everything." Though I made plenty of mistakes and did plenty of dumb things, I'm proud to say there was nothing I did that I would take back if I could—except, of course, my time. You see, and it took me just about twenty-four years to learn this, we only have one life. And the fact that I spent three years wasting that life is something I will never forgive myself for. In fact, if you asked me right now what I did from seventeen to twenty, I couldn't even tell you. I genuinely don't remember what the hell I spent my life doing, except, of course, crying as I made questionable decision after questionable decision and hoping that everything going on around me was just a bad dream. A bad dream that I would eventually wake up from back in Florida, without a torn ankle and thirteen again.

I reconnected with some friends I had grown up with, only to fail miserably as I tried to live a normal teenage life with them. I desperately wanted to do what they were doing and to have fun doing it, as it seemed they were. However, I quickly began to realize I had zero interest in hooking up with strangers or experimenting with drugs, and I had the lowest alcohol tolerance possible (not to mention, I just prefer Vanilla Coke). I watched as people my age wasted away taking drug after drug, remembering how their parents, just yesterday it seemed, were telling mine about their child's Ivy League plans. I spent countless nights as the "mom" to my friends, helping them get home after a rough night of drinking or helping them lie to their parents about their whereabouts. At the same time, my parents were the only parents completely aware of everything I was doing. I think it was a combination of them wanting me to be "normal" and to have a bit of fun after everything I had been through, as well as their confidence in me being a goody two shoes (which I am) that allowed them not to worry about where I was at all hours of the night. Sometimes I wonder how my parents, who, to this day, yell at me to zip up my coat when it's cold outside, let me do half the things that they did. Then again, I'm glad that they did. They trusted me, and although I was out wasting my life away, I knew in the back of my mind that the one thing I could never do was disappoint them.

Those around me confused me. They were always complaining about how worried they were about getting into good colleges and working tirelessly at internships and impressive extracurricular activities, yet ruining their bodies and futures with sex, drugs, and alcohol any chance they could get. It was almost as if they thought that doing the "correct" thing to get into good schools would cancel out the bad luck they were setting themselves up for with their other actions. And that the bad things they were doing were fine as long as they never got caught. And, it was as if listing the multiple internships and opportunities they have taken part in somehow made their troubling and sometimes even illegal actions okay. I guess you could say they were living the lives of future politicians.

I must explain for those who don't know, growing up in New York City is very different when it comes to attending school. By middle school, kids are walking or taking public transportation to school by themselves. In most schools, kids are allowed to go out for lunch to local restaurants in high school or even middle school. We're also surrounded by nightlife and excitement every single day that many others don't get to see in their lifetimes. I remember once hearing from a family friend that they had come to New York and wanted to visit a club called Lavo because they had seen a celebrity spend his birthday there. They told me they waited in the cold for two hours, just to be turned away without getting in. At the same time, a neighbor my age celebrated his eighteenth birthday there, with his parents paying thousands of dollars for tables for his friends. All of his underage friends got in by using fake IDs and tipping the bouncers. This was a normal thing in New York City, yet I'm sure it's unheard of elsewhere around the country. But this was the life of those I grew up with. There were different cliques and groups, of course, like there are anywhere else. But despite some groups spending time in their friends' apartments when their parents weren't home, and other groups spending time at fancy nightclubs, deep down they were all the same. They were teenagers wasting their lives. Sure, they did so in different ways and with different amounts of money, but it all led to the same end result.

It was a life that very quickly turned boring for me. How many times could I watch the same girl throw up at a party? Or "babysit" a group of kids who paid me to make sure they didn't end up dead or seriously hurt while trying mushrooms? Or tell the same people for the thousandth time that I do not, in fact, ever plan on trying marijuana? (And, by the way, I can proudly say I never have.) Every single thing that I had thought I missed out on turned out to be absolute crap. Everything that my own family members were telling me I *needed* to experience turned out to be less exciting than a basic skills figure skating competition. More importantly, it was a waste of time, and to this day, I wonder why so many young people waste away every day by making these same decisions, decisions that everyone around them seems to think are the "normal" thing to do.

It's probably because we're constantly told that our lives don't need to actually be good but just need to look good on paper. Kids as young as twelve and thirteen are even encouraged to make "dumb mistakes" as long as they also have a piece of paper that lists their extracurricular activities on it. And God forbid someone wants to be homeschooled, or begin working in a different environment and in a different way, or to commit their life to a passion in a way most wouldn't. Even if those decisions lead you to make fewer "dumb mistakes," they are still frowned upon. People want you to succeed, but only as much as they could themselves, never more or differently. Remember that. And remember that the piece

of paper with your grades, extracurricular activities, and internships on it doesn't mean anything if you don't like the person you
are. And no, it does not make it okay to waste your life making
stupid mistakes either, even if the world is set on convincing you
that you should be making those mistakes. Of course people want
you to be "normal" and make the same mistakes that they made—
that way you can avoid being different and unique, the one thing
everybody is most terrified of.

I had just lived through three exhilarating years on the ice, and
this teenage lifestyle certainly was not going to fill the void that
my failed skating career had left behind. I was shocked by the lack
of awareness of those around me. These were kids who got perfect
scores on the SATs, kids who ended up going to Ivy League schools,
and kids who interned and worked at top-tier companies while still
in high school. And yet, they were incredibly foolish. There was an
entire world out there full of excitement and adventure, yet all
that excited them was the bottle of Xanax that they found on my
nightstand. Think about that for a second. I was prescribed Xanax
to calm my anxiety and the terrible thoughts I was trying to get out
of my head. And while I was focusing on trying to get myself away
from relying on this medication forever and proud of myself for
not needing it in weeks, the kids around me who had spent the last
three years studying and working and doing the "right" thing were
asking me how much I would sell it for.

It felt as though I had entered the twilight zone. Everybody around me was the same. I had never understood the fun in being normal, and now even more so, I couldn't understand the appeal. Those who didn't try certain drugs or who chose to abstain from sex were made fun of. And those who continued to make the same terrible decisions that those around them were making seemed convinced that it was the right thing to do. Nobody even questioned whether breaking from the pack was a good idea. They just followed each other like sheep, regularly making one bad decision after another. I was confused, frustrated, and extremely disappointed all at once. I had thought I made a big sacrifice when I chose to move to Florida and pursue an athletic career. Though in my heart I knew that it was the right thing to do, my brain worried about all that I would be giving up. Why did I think about this? Because of all the adults around me who told me to. Family, friends, and neighbors all constantly berated my parents for allowing me to live such an unusual and risky life—as if somehow keeping your kids away from drugs is "risky." I had not only learned more in school than everybody I had left behind in the few years that I spent training, but more importantly, I had learned a lot more about the world and myself.

I remember one specific night when we were gathered at my grandparents' house. My cousins were telling me, in their favorite condescending tone, how great this loss of skating was going to be for my future. My aunt threw in a jab about how I may still be able to catch up to others my age in school. "Sports are not a way of life," I was told over and over again. It was as if my parents hadn't made sure that I had taken advantage of being homeschooled for three years, taking all honors classes, getting straight As, and learning Chinese, my fourth language. Everyone around me wanted me to be "normal" so badly that it didn't matter what that even meant. It didn't matter that my education was actually benefitting from being homeschooled and that I was ahead of others my age, it didn't matter that I had been happier than I ever thought I could be for the past three years, and it didn't matter that those my age and attending the school I most likely would have attended had I not moved to Florida to skate were ruining their lives with drugs and alcohol. No, it only mattered that I was different, and they didn't like that. What followed was a conversation about athletes and all sports fans alike because to some people in my family, that's just one giant lump of uneducated, awful people. I hated it. I hated listening to it and being judged by people who couldn't care less about me or anything I was doing. They didn't care for one second that I had lost my life's dream. They didn't stop for two seconds to realize that I had given up my friends, my city, my health, and much more at just eleven years old to pursue a sport and, therefore, how much that sport must mean to me. And they certainly didn't stop to ask how I was doing after all of that had been taken away from me. No, they were just glad I would be "normal" again. Whatever the hell that even means.

6

I've never really believed in the saying, "When one door closes, another one opens," but weirdly enough, that's exactly what happened to me. In the most random of circumstances, I was "discovered" and signed to Wilhelmina Models, one of the top modeling agencies in the entire world, when I was seventeen. And by the way, when I say this was completely random, I think that's an understatement.

Back in Florida, about a year before I suffered the injury that killed my dreams, my mom found a tiny dog outside of the high school where I was taking my standardized tests. She had been waiting outside of the school in our car for about an hour when she says she discovered this dog in the middle of the road behind her. To this day, I have my doubts, because when I tell you this was the most special dog in the world, I'm not kidding. Just the sheer thought that somebody would throw away this perfect little creature still baffles my mind. But somehow, a monster did just that, and God sent this little dog to my mother, who, of course, rescued him immediately and treated him as if he were her long-lost child.

Timmy became a member of the family instantly and, of course, moved back home to New York with us after I got injured. One afternoon, while my mom was walking him in the park, she was approached by a photographer. This photographer had been doing a photo shoot in Central Park and had just found out that the dog that was hired to join the shoot had canceled. Of course, my mom didn't hesitate to let them use Timmy for a few shots, not even asking what magazine the shoot was for. Let me also just add that Timmy was a rare, tri-colored, teddy bear Pomeranian. He was a walking model everywhere he went already, with people chasing us down in the streets begging to pet him from the minute we rescued him and cleaned him up. He had a right to be a cocky little thing, though. When we rescued him, he had three dislocated legs and congestive heart failure, and he was not only the cutest but the toughest little dog there ever was. If you ever saw his precious face, I promise that you would agree that the one place Timmy most definitely belonged was in front of the camera.

We learned that day in the park that there are dogs that work in modeling and/or show business who have their own bank accounts, and because we, of course, did not have one of these set up for Timmy, the photographer had to ask my mom if there was anything else that she could do to return the favor. My mom knew how depressed I was at the time and probably thought that it would be a great experience and an escape from my usual sadness for me to live out every girl's dream for a few hours, so she asked the photographer to do a small photo shoot with me in return. I got ready for what I thought would be my first and last photo shoot, while secretly trying to remember everything I had learned from my years idolizing Tyra Banks and her show, *America's Next Top Model*.

It wasn't that I never wanted to be a model. I genuinely never considered it an option for me, so I never let myself dream about having the opportunity. I won't lie and pretend I never sat in the mirror and practiced my posing while very carefully taking in all of Tyra's advice, but that was the extent of my modeling aspirations. *America's Next Top Model* was my little escape during the last few months of my time in middle school when I first began dealing with bullies. The show let me focus, even if only for an hour a week, on an extravagant and artistic dream that most little girls had at one point or another in their lives. And as a sixteen-year-old girl who had yet to put on any makeup apart from what I had to wear to compete, who never had a boy show any interest in her, and who never had an opportunity to just feel like a teenage girl for a bit, I was pretty damn excited.

The experience was awesome. I felt like a girl, maybe even a powerful one, for the first time in what felt like forever. And already after just those few hours, I was incredibly grateful. But never could I have imagined what was going to come next. About ten days later, the same photographer called me to tell me that she had exciting news. She had sent the images over to Wilhelmina Models, an agency that I had known about from my days of watching *America's Next Top Model* and an agency whose name I never thought would ever come out of my mouth. To my absolute shock, they wanted to work with me.

After two meetings, I was officially a Wilhelmina model. Never in my life did I think that I would get that title. I remember not being able to properly swallow as I would tell people the news. This was a dream I never even knew I had. And yet, when it came true, it felt like I had spent years hoping for it. I remember a small sense of relief washing over me as I closed my eyes the night after we signed the contract. This wasn't relief about the modeling contract, as I had yet to even realize that I had actually just signed one. It was much deeper than that. I felt joy for the first time since I had to say goodbye to skating. And that night, I remember thanking God for the first time in quite a while for everything he had done for me and for the opportunity to feel joy again, something I worried would never happen.

Wilhelmina Models was basically everything that one might think. It was a giant operation in the business of selling flesh to the highest bidder. Yes, it sounds a bit cynical, but I want to tell it like it is. Was modeling incredibly glamorous and exhilarating at times? Of course. But 90 percent of the time, it was every-thing but. My contract had very specific requirements about never changing my appearance. This meant that I wasn't allowed to let my weight fluctuate in any way or to experiment with or have control over my own hair, nails, or skin. They also owned my schedule, requiring me to attend castings regularly and some-times with only a few moments' notice. On top of that, between every new contract that was signed with every job I had, more and more companies and strangers had ownership over my face, which, when you think about it, is incredibly creepy. And yet, I didn't have a problem with any of these things. In a way, I was reminded of my time on the ice. Surrounded by sharks, whether it was fellow models, agents, bookers, or clients, it didn't feel like anyone had my best interest at heart.

There were days when I couldn't tell what was real and what wasn't. Different models would often tell me stories of the horrors that they had experienced, either at the hands of clients or their own agents, and all my seventeen-year-old naïve self could do was listen in awe to the stories about the life that I was now a part of. I was in my own little James Bond movie all over again, and the high from those experiences kept me going for quite some time. Between the obsession with selfies, Soul Cycle, and kale, I was in a world I found quite entertaining, even including some of the pretty insane stuff I was surrounded by. In fact, I'm a lot more disgusted now than I ever was in the moment. Unfortunately, that explains why so many models are "discovered," plucked from their homes, and sold to different companies and clients as young teenagers: they are still too young to understand everything going on around them.

Was I confident in my appearance? I was getting there. But being forced to strip off most of your clothing and walk around an office in nothing but your heels and a bikini (or bra and underwear for some) takes a level of confidence that I had no idea people could attain, certainly not me. Every visit to my agent had to start or end with new "digitals" as they were called. Meaning, we would stand in our bikinis or underwear (I always chose a bikini or sports bra) and get new images taken of us standing against one of the blank walls in the office. These images were then stored in our file and used, along with our portfolios, by our agents and bookers to try and get us jobs. In the moment it may have felt strange, but it was something I had to do. And as uncomfortable as I was at the start, that's exactly where I learned that confidence is not something you are born with but rather something you must work to attain. I quickly learned I had to "fake it till I make it" and let myself naturally gain the type of confidence that bullied middle school Elizabeth never could have imagined having.

On one of my first jobs, I experienced one of my favorite moments of my entire life. It was the kind of moment that reminds you that there certainly is a God and that He is, in fact, looking out for you. I was booked for a fitness modeling job in Pennsylvania and remember getting on the bus early in the morning, eager to begin my short nap on the way over there. Of course, what my agent forgot to tell me was that there would be a male model, also from Wilhelmina, joining me at the shoot that day. He got on the bus, noticed me, and asked, "Wilhelmina?" I nodded, filled with confidence knowing that a seasoned male model could tell just by looking at me that I was a model with a top agency, and nuzzled back into the pillow I had fashioned out of my hoodie and backpack. Upon closing my eyes, I started to realize that he looked extremely familiar and wondered where I could have possibly met this beautiful person before. Luckily, my exhaustion that morning was a lot stronger than my need to remember this model's name, and I drifted off to sleep without getting to spend another moment thinking about him.

Two hours later, we arrived in Pennsylvania, making small talk as we waited in the bus station to get picked up. He was very nice and extremely confident, certainly more confident and manly than any guy I had met in my life. I was just excited to be spending the day with him, already forgetting that I was in Pennsylvania to work. During lunch a few hours later, we began talking, and it hit me. About five years ago, when the bullying in my school had gotten really bad, this male model was a tiny part of making everything okay.

Let me elaborate. In seventh grade, my mom made an agreement with my school in New York and the Board of Education of New York State. Because I was already training on the ice before and after school and getting in well above my necessary hours of physical education, I could skip gym class. This meant that I could use the hour that I would have been stuck in the class to catch up on homework instead. I had been waking up at three-thirty in the morning every day to skate before school and then heading back for a two-hour practice after school. This left me very little time to get all of my homework done, so every extra minute I could get was a big help. Of course, the other kids thought this was unfair, with many going as far as to accuse me and my family of lying about my skating schedule and targeting me with mean-girl tactics that seemed directly out of a bad high school movie.

Thinking back, those girls deserve some credit for how elaborate their evil plan was. You see, they knew that I had to leave school at exactly 4 p.m., and not a minute later, in order to make it to my afternoon practice, which was over an hour away. So, they damaged some of their own belongings, blamed it on me, and had the school require that I sit with a counselor weekly after we were dismissed to try to get through whatever issues they made them believe I was dealing with. The principal knew that they had been bullying me for weeks because my parents had complained to her on more than one occasion. But apparently, realizing that this was a part of some middle school mean-girl plan was much less convincing than just believing that I had snapped and destroyed the belongings of my bullies.

On one particular day, I remember walking home after school with Lidunia after another useless hour with the school counselor. My skating was falling behind, and all I could think about was all the practice that I was missing while dealing with the nonsense of the bullies around me. I cried the entire walk home that day, fed up with the world and how cruel I was slowly realizing people were and looking forward to the one thing that I knew could lighten my mood. This was a Wednesday afternoon, and on every Wednesday afternoon, at 5 p.m. sharp, there was a new episode of *America's Next Top Model*, my favorite show. I remember walking home in tears that day, telling myself that, in a matter of moments, I would be sitting on the couch, watching my hour with Tyra Banks and getting to disappear into a fantasy world of elegance and extravagance. That evening, as I wiped my tears and the episode began, Tyra introduced a male model that the contestants would be working with. He was so confident and suave and everything I imagined a superstar to be. And now, five years later, he was sitting on a studio floor, eating lunch with me on a job, as a fellow Wilhelmina model.

Even though being a part of this extravagant world came with confidence and strength that I never knew I would feel, it also brought with it many internal struggles. The body that I had grown up with very quickly disappeared when I stopped training. I had to get used to not only weighing about fifty pounds more and growing six inches what felt like overnight but also being viewed very differently. Almost immediately after getting injured and stopping my training, I grew the boobs that I had prayed for as a bullied middle school student and the butt and thighs I never wanted. I knew that in the modeling world (much like in the real world), everything was based on looks. My appearance dictated the kind of jobs that I would get, something I very quickly had to learn. Within a few months, I wasn't even getting booked for the fitness modeling that I had originally been signed for. I was modeling as a woman because that's what I looked like, and I had to learn to love it.

Growing up in a world where any physical changes are frowned upon is very difficult. When I was skating, I not only had to make sure I didn't gain any weight but also had to try to do whatever the internet told me to do in terms of stunting my growth. So, accepting the fact that everything had changed was hard for me. I would walk the streets of New York and deal with catcalling on every corner. I knew that I did (and still do) have the face of a twelve-year-old, and yet, I was getting disgusting attention everywhere I went from men who, just a year ago, wouldn't have looked my way. I felt like I had aged ten years in just a few months and was desperately trying to accept what I had become. So, I turned to the opportunity that God had handed me and I let modeling give me the power and self-confidence that I knew it could give me if I just allowed it to. I had to learn to accept my new body one way or another and decided what better opportunity than in an industry focused around beauty, one that I'm so insanely lucky to even get to be a part of?

This didn't come without its share of internal struggles, though. I remember on one occasion a photographer I trusted told me, "You can't be a good model and a virgin. It's just impossible." I went home that night and told my parents I was done. If someone thought that I would have to give my body to someone in order to sell a bathing suit or an article of clothing, I knew that it was not an industry I wanted to be a part of. But just like my amazing mother had done when I was told that there was no way I could become a competitive figure skater by starting as late as I did, she sat with me as I cried my eyes out in insecurity and very quickly built me back up.

If the world thought that I needed to have sex with someone in order to feel good enough about myself to sell an article of clothing, then I was going to have to change the world. I wanted to be able to feel beautiful and sexy like so many other girls my age, but that was not the way I was going to accomplish it. So instead of trying to change myself in order to be a better model, I decided to use modeling to create a better sense of self. I knew that modeling was not going to last forever, and I wanted the chance to use the opportunities I was getting in order to feel good about who I was becoming.

It would have been so, so easy to let myself become someone else and to gain only negative things from my experiences in the modeling world. It's easy in the fashion industry to become everything from super insecure to super narcissistic, depending on how you let different experiences shape who you become. It's a complicated world and one that can change you in ways you never thought you could be changed if you let it. My dad taught me when I was very young that there is something to learn from everyone and everything, and that's exactly what I was ready to do. I knew the negative effects that modeling could have on my mental health and my life. But I also knew about the positive effects, and those are the ones I was going to experience, because that was what I knew I needed.

I know most of you reading this right now have seen many of the photo shoots and jobs that I got to take part in. Unfortunately, or maybe fortunately, the ones that get reposted on the internet are never the most appropriate ones, and I always get stuck feeling as though I must explain myself. So, I will right now, for the last and final time. Number one, I don't believe in judging anybody. I genuinely cannot stand judgmental people. Thinking that you know everything about a person from looking at them, or worse, looking at just a photo of them, is incredibly irritating. I've met a lot of people in my life, from all over the world and from many different industries. If I hadn't, I would probably be a much more judgmental person myself, as it's easy to be one when you think you know and have seen it all. But since I have, I know for a fact that I know absolutely nothing about anyone, what they believe in, or what they have been through until I meet them. I refuse to let anyone's appearance, vocation, political affiliation, age, race, sexuality, or anything else guide me in making a quick judgment. I don't believe in that, and I don't let myself spend time with anyone who does. Before I started modeling, I'm sure that I would have been someone who looked at a model's images and thought that I had a right to call her names or assume something about her personality. Thank God I've experienced enough to not be that person, which is more than I can say for many people in my life, and unfortunately, many people around the world.

Second, when I started modeling, I was incredibly insecure. I was bullied quite a bit for my unibrow, my hair, my lack of chest, and countless other things in elementary and middle school. And although I genuinely never thought it bothered me, I learned many years later that it had. When I began modeling, I had yet to go on a date. Girls around me were constantly talking about who they were going out with, and I didn't even feel comfortable enough in myself as a woman to consider attempting to go on a date with someone (not that anyone was asking, either). I felt uncomfortable in my own skin as a woman, and without modeling, I don't think I could have ever gotten over that, especially knowing the confidence issues that I still struggle with today.

Third, modeling and showing more or less skin does not mean anything at all about who you are as a person, plain and simple. In fact, I think it means the opposite. Owning your body and deciding what you do with it is extremely powerful. It's a much different power from the one that comes with deciding who to give your body to. For me, modeling swimwear or lingerie meant taking charge of my own body instead of giving it to others. Modeling actually kept me much tamer and more innocent because I learned my own worth and what it would mean to share a piece of that with someone. If you are close-minded enough to think that you know what a person does in their private life because they modeled in a lingerie catalog, then you have a lot of learning to do.

Fourth, I have the most incredible dad in the world, and I trust him with my life. He is not only the smartest person alive but also the most decent, and as his daughter, I have no bigger fear than disappointing him. When I began modeling and showing him images, I realized how much more his opinion meant to me than those of any of my agents or the clients and companies that I worked for. I vowed to never let a provocative image get published without his approval first, a promise that I have proudly kept. My dad knows me, and more importantly, he knows the world that we are in. He has been through enough and seen enough to understand that somebody cannot be judged by anything except the content of their character. I knew he would never judge me or assume something about my character from a photo, unlike many family members and friends of mine. I also knew of his expectations for me, which I take incredibly seriously. I knew that he would always share his opinion and make sure that his daughter was shown in the best light, something he did and still does with every photo shoot and job, no matter how small. And I knew that he would build me up every single time, making sure I knew that I was allowed to feel beautiful and not let anybody tell me otherwise. My dad was like my unofficial agent during my modeling career, making sure that everything was done according to his standards (which are pretty high if I may add). If he believes that we stuck to every standard that he had for me, as a team, then I have zero regrets. Plain and simple.

Lastly, modeling and religion do not intertwine in my head. My religion guides me, and if I thought I shouldn't be a part of the modeling world, then I wouldn't be. Do I judge others who choose to be more or less modest when it comes to their clothing or the photos that they take? Of course not. And I hope that I would get the same respect in return (though I know better than to assume that is the case). I have my own relationship with God, one that I take incredibly seriously and one that I never want to lose. When I choose to keep kosher or attend synagogue on Shabbat, I do it because I know it is the right thing to do for me. It is what I know God expects of me, and I could never consider letting Him down. But do I judge others who do anything differently? Never. I am a proud practicing Jew. And I genuinely feel as though that is displayed in my actions. If someone doesn't see that, that is not my problem. I answer to Hashem and nobody else.

7

While I will always look back at my modeling career positively, that doesn't mean I didn't also experience my fair share of not-so-positive adventures. Imagine constantly being looked at and treated like an object. Imagine being used as a human coat hanger for jobs with people thinking they can dress you how they like and undress you when they like. Imagine working with photographers who feel comfortable asking you to change in front of them or who pressure you to undress more and more for photo shoots. It's not always fun. And I can't even remember how many photographers tried to bully me into thinking that undressing for them would somehow help my career. The first ten times were pretty stressful, but eventually you get used to it. Standing up for myself was not something I was always able to do, but it's something I learned how to do pretty quickly after enough people told me to undress for them or "face the consequences." These photographers weren't nobodies, by the way. They were extremely well known in the industry and continue to work today.

I remember one photographer in particular who asked me to do a "test shoot" with him. Photographers often do test shoots with models where the images aren't paid for or meant to be published in a magazine, but they can instead be used by both the model and photographer in their portfolios. With social media getting more and more popular and Instagram accounts becoming people's public portfolios, more and more photographers and models are now regularly messaging each other over the app to arrange these test shoots. So, when this photographer asked if I wanted to shoot with him, and I saw all of the well-known models and celebrities he had photographed, I jumped at the opportunity. After our first conversation, I was ecstatic thinking about the fact that I would get to work with such a well-known and well-connected photographer. And then during our second conversation, I realized how ridiculous I was for assuming this photographer might actually be a decent person who wanted to work with me for the right reasons.

When I asked him to tell me what date and time could work for him, he followed his answer up with "and you'll also shoot for my new coffee table book, ok?" For a millisecond I thought this photographer was about to include me in a big, exciting project of his, possibly my big break, and again I was ecstatic. But after asking what this coffee table book project was, I learned how mistaken I was. "It'll be just topless shots," he told me. I tried to kindly explain that I had not shot nude and never planned to, but that I was thankful for his consideration. He responded by telling me that unless I agreed to shoot nude for this private book of his, he was uninterested in working with me in any capacity. Of course, in that moment, I realized how much of a creep this person was. When I later googled him, I found out he had been accused of not just harassment, but sexual assault against multiple women; and yet he was still getting work from high-level models and celebrities.

Looking back, I'm not sure why I was surprised by any of this. When I was seventeen and had just signed my Wilhelmina contract, a man who claimed to be a model "scout" reached out to me after seeing me on the agency's website. He was extremely kind and respectful, and being the naïve and innocent teenager that I was, I found no reason not to meet with him. After going out for what I felt was an innocent and normal meeting at a coffee shop, he texted me his demands—a blowjob every time he was in New York, for the modeling campaign of my choice. And regular sex with him if I chose to accompany him on any of his fancy getaways to different fashion shows and events. He also threw in the fact that being a part of these "getaways" would be vital for my career and success as a model. Luckily, I escaped from both of these creeps unharmed, but can only imagine what could have happened if I somehow ended up alone with them at any point.

Elizabeth Pipko

Some adventures, I can tell you, seem a hell of a lot scarier in hindsight, and thank God for that! A few months ago, I was sitting at home reading the news about R. Kelly. The allegations made against him had become unavoidable, with everyone you spoke to asking if you had watched *Surviving R. Kelly*, the documentary depicting some of his disgusting actions. Out of nowhere, a memory appeared in my mind. In 2013, all of the models at my agency were invited to a holiday party held at a famous nightclub in New York City. Since many of the models were under twenty-one, me included, we were given bracelets to let the bartenders know we were underage. The minute we stepped inside, an agent I barely knew came over and ripped the bracelet off my hand. She winked at me and continued to do the same for other underage girls. I didn't think much of it in the moment, except that they wanted us to have fun. To this day, I never like to have more than one drink in a single night, so I wasn't worried about myself, just intrigued by how open these agents were about breaking these rules. At around eleven, the party ended but the club remained open for the public, and we noticed that there were celebrities everywhere. Out of nowhere they all appeared, and as I looked around, I saw a sign that read "Black Panties" in large foil balloons. A few minutes later, another model explained to me that the evening was now turning into the album release party for R. Kelly's new album, *Black Panties*. Do I have some stories about the craziness that I saw that night? Yes. Am I incredibly glad that I got tired by midnight and went home? Definitely. Just to think that these were the situations that we, as young models, were put in regularly leaves a bad taste in my mouth. I may have felt like an adult in the moment, but it's quite unnerving to look back, knowing that I was really just a child who was thrown into one of the craziest industries around, and sometimes in incredibly dangerous situations. Still, modeling gave me a glimpse into the true darkness of our world—a darkness that exists in every industry and, despite its reputation, is certainly not exclusive to the modeling world.

Even during my days at Wilhelmina, with all the excitement going on around me, I was still the same person deep down: a girl who had lost herself and her dream and was desperate to find it again. I was trying to be like everyone else and learning very quickly that I, in fact, did not enjoy most people's activities of choice. However, I did learn something about myself that I genuinely would not have known otherwise. And that is that everybody, me included, wants to be loved. At twelve years old, I laughed at other skaters when they told me about their crushes. No relationship was ever going to matter more to me than skating, and I couldn't understand how the girls I skated with even had the time to daydream about celebrity crushes instead of the Olympic rings. Years later, I would sit in the waiting room at castings and roll my eyes as I heard some of the most beautiful women in the world talk about how much they wanted to be in relationships and get married. I often even laughed at characters in movies when they obsessed over a boy who they thought they were in love with. And yet, when it began to happen to me, it was as if all reality completely went out the window.

When you're a teenage girl, boys are often on your mind. And when you're a seventeen-year-old girl who is watching everyone go on dates and realize that you yourself haven't even interacted with anyone of the opposite sex apart from family members and coaches in a few years, it certainly begins to take up a significant part of your thoughts. Now that I look back, I'm not sure if it had to be this particular boy in order to have the effect on me that it did. Sometimes I think that a first love is a first love no matter who it is and how they treat you. This was certainly the case for me. I would love to spare you the details of any relationship that was formed, not because I want to keep any of it a secret, but because I'm afraid to say there was nothing there to even tell you about. This was an on-and-off relationship that lasted four years, which is about four years longer than it ever should have gone on. I was asked out on a date, at sixteen, for the first time in my life, and what followed were years of confusion and emotional abuse. This was abuse of a teenage girl who had no idea she was being treated improperly by, sadly, a boy who was not much older and who probably did not even realize that he was guilty. Unfortunately, the real story is not in the relationship itself, but in the effect it had on me.

Now when I think about it, I'm pretty confident I was anything but in love with this person. However, in the moment, I was completely convinced that I was. And sadly, there isn't much difference between being in love and thinking that you're in love, at least when it comes to the effects on your body. I was overwhelmed and excited, but more importantly—for the first time in what felt like a very, very long time—I was distracted. Suddenly, skating wasn't the only thing on my mind, and it was a good feeling. I wasn't crying myself to sleep or harming myself, and that seemed like a pretty great improvement at the time. I realize, looking back, that my addictive personality probably just needed something new to become addicted to, and that it was not love or anything to be taken seriously. However, as they say, hindsight is always twenty-twenty. And though it may seem like an innocent teenage love story, this was one that cost me quite a bit.

All of the anxiety I had learned to manage during skating came flooding back. All of a sudden, everything I knew how to control as an athlete became unmanageable. It was as if I had entered into a world I had never been in before. Even my experiences at photo shoots couldn't compare to the out-of-body anxiety I felt when thinking about this person. Out of nowhere, I was feeling butterflies in my stomach because of someone's texts and calls. Little did I know, those butterflies would eventually turn into something a lot more serious. For anyone reading this, please heed my warning and respect yourself. At the first sign of someone not knowing your worth, just walk away. I learned the hard way that it's much more difficult to walk away after the tenth or fifteenth red flag than it could have been after the first.

I don't know what it was that caused me to react the way that I did. I had never been disrespected that way or that often by somebody before. In fact, whether it came to bullies in middle school or competitors on the ice, I never had any problem defending myself to anyone. I knew who I was and what I deserved, and I often spoke out, even when unnecessary, if it meant defending myself or someone I loved. And yet, I let him get away with everything. From the name-calling to the lies, I treated everything as if it were my fault and proceeded to let myself get more anxious by the day. Eventually, the anxiety got the best of me and turned much worse than just sweating and stomach pains. I began vomiting daily, not able to control my nerves and not realizing what it was doing to my health. I stopped eating completely. People ask me why this happened, and I still cannot figure it out. It was not an attempt to lose weight or to alter my appearance in any way; at least it wasn't a conscious one. It was more of an angst that took over my entire body and kept me from being able to eat anything or live a healthy life. Eventually, my stomach shrunk to a point where I couldn't consume any food. When I look back, I can clearly see that I allowed someone to distract me from my sadness for a short period of time, only to later fall right back into my misery—a misery that was now not only about skating, but about this relationship. I remember one morning trying to eat the eggs my mom had made and realizing I could not go on like this any longer. I loved her scrambled eggs and had woken up craving them that day. And yet, every time I attempted to swallow a piece, my body refused to let me. That was what the relationship that I had created inside my own head and allowed to go on the way that it had for so long was doing to me.

The magical relationship that I had convinced myself could be a reality turned out to be a crazy illusion. An illusion that messed with my heart, my head, and my health for so long that it probably left me with some lifelong ramifications. More importantly, it was an illusion that I created inside my own head to distract myself from the sadness I felt about losing my dream. But no matter who I brought into my life, they couldn't fill the void that skating left. In fact, they only made me miss it more.

I think it's important to point out that while I was no longer skating, completely shutting it out of my brain was practically impossible. Though I probably looked as though all was fine with my health, I was still recovering from the ankle injury that I had suffered. I was taking medication for inflammation and pain and was constantly trying new procedures to see what could help with the discomfort. At the same time, I was in physical therapy three days a week, just learning to walk up and down the stairs again— super fun, I know. Every time I set foot into the physical therapy center, the doctor's office, the emergency room, the X-ray center, or the acupuncturist's office, I felt the same sinking feeling in my gut. I couldn't go one day without a reminder of everything I had lost and everything that I missed so terribly. Is this a good excuse for ruining four years of my life because of a guy who treated me like scum? Definitely not. But I'm learning to be easier on myself in order to get over some of the mistakes I made. Hopefully, if I can learn to forgive myself, maybe I'll one day stop looking back at the time I let some guy take my dignity away from me. Luckily, I still have the anxiety disorder and recurring stomach ulcers to remind me either way!

I'm sure you're wondering right now, why is this relevant information? Well, I was a girl who lost what felt like everything. I was sad and alone and spent my days literally cutting shapes into my arm with a razor to pass the time and dull my sadness. I had no friends and what felt like nothing to look forward to. And at the same time, I allowed myself to be sucked into a relationship that drove me to an eating disorder and a job that only encouraged all of this erratic and dangerous behavior. I remember dealing with this guy on the same day that I had gone in to see my agent and show him some new portfolio images that I had shot with my friend (also a model at Wilhelmina). I read the message from the guy I was seeing, "Well, if you don't want to have sex, this isn't worth it to me," and turned off my phone.

A few minutes later, my agent was calling my friend and me "slutty sorority girls" and telling us everything that was wrong with the photos and our appearances. After about an hour of being torn apart we were introduced to a new booker our agent had hired. We were used to having female bookers at that point; generally, many modeling agents are females or gay males, which usually makes young models feel a lot more comfortable. But this new booker was the opposite of anything that could make anyone feel more comfortable. He was a recent college grad and a fraternity brother, something he mentioned quite a bit. And now, he had access to photos of me in lingerie—how wonderful. My gut told me the direction that this was going to go, and within a few days, I was proven correct. This booker took the numbers of both my friend and I out of the system and began texting us and asking us to meet up with him for coffee. Eventually, it turned into messages saying, "Meet me for dinner tomorrow, and I can make sure you get into that casting." Soon he was bullying me online, very similarly to the guy who had caused me to lose ten pounds, and I was sick of it. I remember waking up to a comment of his on one of my Instagram pictures saying, "You can't make me put any of this in your portfolio, but you can throw whatever nonsense you want up here!" I was shocked. Why was this allowed? And from an agent of young girls?

Confronting the staff at Wilhelmina did not work out as I expected. What I thought would be a casual meeting between me and the lead agent in charge of the agency ended up with me being cornered into an office with her and the agent I was there to complain about. I sat there as I was bullied for an hour. I was told I wasn't working enough, even though I had booked more jobs that summer than any season before. I also had to listen to them tell me that I wasn't pretty enough to be a model. That's right. I went in to complain to the head of a modeling agency that I had worked with for over two years to tell them about how I was being bullied and sexually harassed. And they responded by telling me that I was never pretty enough to be a model anyway and that I was lucky I had been in the building for as long as I had. I don't know what they expected me to do when this garbage started, but staying around to be sexually harassed and bullied wasn't what was going to happen. That day I was terminated for not letting someone regularly harass me, and I was damn proud of it. They violated most of my contract with their actions. More importantly, they illegally terminated my contract, which was supposed to go on for another year. But what was done was done. And it was what

God wanted for me. I stood up and turned to my agent. "I'll still be on the cover of every magazine. It just won't happen with you," I said. And I walked away with my head held higher than ever before. It didn't matter if it was this agent, or the guy I was dumb enough to date, or anyone else. Nobody was going to mess with me anymore.

8

Feeling like myself again was a great change. And yes, most of it came from finally standing up for myself after what felt like too many years of tears. However, there was another reason that I was feeling a tiny bit more like myself.

Let me back up a bit. While I was sitting in my cast and feeling more miserable than ever, my parents decided that it would be a good idea to take me to watch a skating competition. Did it seem evil and crazy at the time? Hell yes. But I had nothing else going on. So, I took a break from my regularly scheduled programming of crying and complaining and went with them. This was a senior-level international competition at my local rink with top-level skaters representing countries around the world. Of course, I sat there pretending to be disinterested because I knew if I focused too much on everything going on, I would begin to cry. Plus, I was starting to get some pretty excruciating headaches from all the crying I had been doing and knew it was time I put a conscious effort into stopping. While I sat and stared off into the distance and played with my hair, I suddenly heard, "She represents the Israeli Federation." It was as if everything stopped in that moment. Yes, I sound crazy dramatic, but this moment is so ingrained in my mind, that is the only way to describe it.

I remember seeing two people holding Israeli flags in the audience. I don't remember how the girl skated or anything else that was going on. But I remember seeing them and then looking up and asking God, "If you fix my ankle, I will come back and do this for all of us." I had a new dream—probably one of the craziest I've had, but it was a dream. So yes, I may have spent three years crying about my failed career, but I never gave up hope. As soon as I began physical therapy, I began secretly training. I've made many mistakes and starting out as quickly as I did was probably one of them. But it's hard for me to regret something that makes me so undeniably happy. Wollman Rink, the ice-skating rink in Central Park, which is about five minutes from my apartment, is one of the reasons I was able to come back to the ice. I knew how scared my parents would be if I told them that I was defying all doctors' orders and skating again, but I also knew that nobody was going to believe in me until I showed them that I could do it. And how could I show them if they didn't let me try? I began sneaking out of our apartment early in the morning without my parents knowing and skating short sessions. I also began jogging in the park when they thought I was doing something else. Slowly but surely, I was going to come back to what I loved, no matter the pain.

Let me quickly explain the medical situation before the haters say that I faked an injury (as many have claimed I faked an entire skating career). I tore three ligaments, two tendons, and three-quarters of my Achilles tendon. I also fractured or bruised most of the bones in my foot. Luckily, almost everything healed except for one ligament, which never grew back together. I was offered to have it surgically re-attached but was then told by many doctors that that would restrict the range of motion in my ankle and make it even harder for me to even wear competitive skates again, let alone attempt a comeback. So after my injury and years of physical therapy, medications, and different treatments, I am left with a ligament that never grew back together, tendinitis in my ankle, and lots of pain and inflammation that intensifies whenever it's cold or raining or I choose to walk more than fifteen blocks. It could definitely be much worse! But this is the opposite of ideal for a figure skater, especially as it is the ankle of the leg that I land all of my jumps on. So, was it going to be impossible to come back? Probably not! But was it going to cause excruciating pain, yup! However, I was completely ready for that. What I wasn't ready for was the emotional pain that it caused, but I'll get to that in a bit.

I waited until I had worked out for about half a year before I told my parents or any doctors. Eventually I was told that what I was doing was dangerous, but as long as I could deal with the agonizing pain and knew the risks that could come from injuring my ankle again, I was cleared to skate. I was given some medication for inflammation and pain, which I relied on quite heavily for the first year. Some days I added five or six Advil on top of the inflammation medication—not ideal, but I was skating again, which was all that mattered to me. I had already proven more than ten doctors wrong with what I was able to do, and now, about six years later, I'm finally realizing that I should be proud of myself for that alone. But at the same time that I was attempting to skate at a basic skills level again, I was also doing something incredibly special: becoming an Israeli citizen.

I am probably the proudest American that you will ever meet (apart from my brother). But after I came home from that competition and sat on the floor of my room begging God to fix my ankle, I knew what I wanted to do. Skating had taken on a new meaning for me, and it was about so much more than just an athletic career this time. That night, I watched a documentary on the Munich massacre (the attack during the 1972 Summer Olympics where Palestinian terrorist group Black September took eleven Israeli Olympic team members hostage and killed them) and knew exactly what I needed to do. If I was going to put my all into a comeback to this sport, I was going to do it representing Israel. This isn't about picking one country over another. In fact, the Olympics and any real competitions were so unattainable for me that, in that moment, I wasn't even thinking about something like that. I was thinking of my grandfather and what this would mean to him. I was thinking of the Jewish people, who have been put through so much for no reason except their religious identity. And I was thinking of how much it would mean to be able to come back to this sport after what I was told was a career-ending injury and look up into the crowd at a competition and see the flag of the Jewish state. This was for something a lot bigger than my skating aspirations, and it was something that I simply felt I had to do.

Let me say this loud and clear: the United States is my home. It is the single greatest country in the world, and the country that has allowed me to remain a gigantic patriot while also being a proud Jew and supporter of Israel, something not possible almost anywhere else in the world. My love for the United States of America is unparalleled; it's that simple. But in that moment, I felt as though this was what God wanted for me. It gave skating a different meaning for me, something it had never meant before. It was for everybody who was stripped of their chance at competing in the 1972 Olympic Games because of the despicable hate that people have for the Jewish people, a hate that remains even today. And it was for the people of Israel, a country built on the kind of love and strength that can only come with God. A country of miracles, warriors, heroes, love, determination, grit, and undeniable power. A country I'm so proud to love and support.

It was even more special for me because of a story that my dad often reminded me of growing up. When my dad and grandmother left the Soviet Union to come to the United States, all of their documents were sent to Israel, as they were for all the Jews who escaped. So, when my dad arrived in New York, immediately applied to Columbia University in June of 1981, and was accepted two months later, he was faced with an issue. Before he could attend Columbia, he would need to provide proof of his previous schooling. What's more, this needed to be done in three weeks' time, but all of his documents were still in Israel. He was told that it would take six months to get the documents to the U.S., so it was suggested that he go to the Israeli consulate and speak with somebody there for help. There, he told me, he was immediately reprimanded for choosing to go to the United States instead of Israel. He said that he stood there and pleaded with them to help him as a fellow Jew, but they refused, and he was forced to leave empty-handed. However, exactly three weeks later, at 8 a.m. sharp, he received a call from the consulate.

"Mr. Pipko, your documents are here. We hope you make us proud as a good Jew and a good student," said a voice on the line. He knew how they felt about his choices and his situation, and still they found it in their hearts to not only help him but to do so in time for him to attend school. And about thirty years later, here I was, in the same Israeli consulate, applying for citizenship.

I filled out all of the forms before my eighteenth birthday. I knew I had to wait until then to sign the final forms without parental consent but wanted to get a head start on the process in order to inform my parents on my eighteenth birthday once the process was complete. Shockingly, despite some concerns from my dad, they were quite supportive of my crazy new dream. I barely had to say two words to explain myself. My mom can look in my eyes and know what I'm feeling, and I knew within two seconds of telling her about my new plans that she would be on board. She's a superhero in every sense of the word. The summer of my birthday, she packed her bags and flew with me to Israel to complete the entire process. She helped me get my paperwork in a matter of days and reminded me on the hour that she not only believed in my ability to make this comeback but that I would be better than I ever was before. Despite my smiling face, she knew I was terrified, and she reassured me every step of the way.

Coming back to skating was incredibly difficult. All I can remember from the first year are tears. The pain, both emotional and physical, was excruciating. It was so bad that I actually don't regret turning down a chance in the 2014 Olympics because I know I couldn't have done it. I rarely say that I can't do something, especially when it comes to tolerating pain, but this was a kind I had never experienced before and never anticipated having to go through.

Elizabeth Pipko

As soon as I had the paperwork finished for my citizenship, my mom and I met with the head of the Israeli figure skating team. He told me that a skater on one of their pair teams, who had already qualified for a spot on the Olympic team, had broken her leg and would be unable to compete. Pair skating is different from the regular singles events. Because pair teams have to do special moves like lifts and throws, their individual elements are much easier than those of a single skater. Meaning that if I could have come back to where I was before I had gotten injured, I would be fine as long as I also spent the months leading up to the Olympic Games learning the specific pair elements that I had never done before. It was an honor to have this opportunity presented to me, but I knew that it was going to be too much. I had no idea if I was going to be able to immediately skate at the level where I had left off, and I was terrified at the idea of pair skating. Pair skaters need to be about five to seven inches apart in height, and despite my height of five-foot-seven being pretty tall for a figure skater, the person who they wanted me to partner with was about six-foot-two, so it could have worked out. But the idea of going through the types of falls that pair skaters deal with while being tossed around by someone that tall and after having spent so many years in and out of the hospital already was something I just could not imagine doing. I dreamed for years of someone even saying the word "Olympics" to me. And yet here I was, with the opportunity right in front of me, knowing that it was something that my body just would not be able to handle.

I turned down the opportunity, and thank God that I did! Because let me tell you, I freakin' sucked. Coming back to skating has been the absolute toughest thing I have had to go through—mentally, physically, and emotionally. I'm proud to say, almost ten years after my injury, I am on the ice almost every day—something I could not be happier about. I love skating more than I've ever loved anything, and not being able to skate hurts me in a way I have yet to figure out how to put into words. My injury healed as best it could, but the physical, emotional, and mental scars that it left me with have been incredibly difficult to deal with. My goal when coming back started out with trying to get all of my double jumps back and to begin working on some triples within a year. Eventually, I learned that that was definitely not going to be the case, and my goal turned into, "Please, no crying today."

I've grown a lot since then. My first year or so back on the ice was spent skating in circles with tears in my eyes. I was always in pain—always. And when I wasn't, I was struggling with the anxiety that came with trying to jump again. Certain days, my body would give in to the anxiety so much that I would leave the ice trembling and struggling to breathe. Other days, I would push myself to fight it, only to end up vomiting into a trash can right behind the boards on the rink. Even on days when I managed to push myself, I would take it too far and go right back to my old ways of harming myself when I couldn't get myself to attempt a jump. On my twenty-first birthday, I swore to myself that I would try my double axel. I had finally begun to start jumping again and pushed myself to the extreme in order to try and land this jump in time for my birthday. I was practically living on Advil at the time, sometimes taking up to fifteen pills a day in order to deal with the pain. I felt as though I wanted and needed to do this jump in order to be proud of myself. The double axel is the jump that causes terrifying flashbacks every time I step into it. It is the only jump that takes off forward, already terrifying for many, and also, it was the jump that I injured myself doing. Every time I step forward to take off, I flash back to the day when I was fifteen and my life completely changed. Every single time.

That entire session was a blur and after two hours on the ice, I found myself sitting in a bathroom stall, crying to my brother on the phone, and slicing at parts of my arm with an old screw I had found on the bathroom floor. I think it's safe to say that was not one of my favorite birthdays. I have found myself in that same position many times in the last few years. Luckily, it is now happening less and less, proving to me that, if nothing else, I am improving mentally at handling everything to do with my sport. On the other hand, my physical pain is now tolerable on most days. When I first came back, there were days where the cold and pressure on my ankle would force me to cancel practice completely. I can now happily tell you that has not happened to me in quite some time. And by the time that this book comes out, I'm hopeful that I'll be able to say it isn't happening at all.

I've tried everything to deal with the emotions that come with being on the ice again. I was a great figure skater, I know that. The problem is, nobody else does. I've always been extremely insecure. I've dealt with confidence issues in every single aspect of my life, but figure skating was my thing. It was the one thing I was good at. On the ice was where I found myself and discovered a love for myself that I otherwise would not have ever had. And on the ice was the one place in the world where I had zero inhibitions, the one place in the world where I remember comfortably and proudly being able to be myself. And now, all of that is gone. It's like I have been slowly trying to convince myself that the girl I knew at twelve, the girl who wouldn't let anything or anyone in the world stop her, is somewhere inside of me still today. Some days I cannot help but sit and wonder how disappointed twelve-year-old Elizabeth would be in me and my fears and worries today. It's been a very tough road, but I'll get there. I know I will—hopefully by the time you're reading this book!

When I tell anyone about my injuries, I am constantly told how tough I am. And before I came back, I probably would have agreed that some of those injuries were extremely difficult to get through, making me seem pretty damn tough. However, I can honestly tell you that what I'm doing now is harder than anything I could have ever imagined doing for this sport when I was twelve. And let me just throw in the fact that I have fractured my right ankle twice since coming back. And yet, going through this comeback has been worse than any injury I could have imagined—yes, even worse than any break, tear, or even a blade to the head. I came back to the ice as a different person. Everything I had been through, both related to my skating life and my personal life, had changed me. This is normal, life changes all the time, and we can never be prepared for what comes with it. But this is why skaters are so successful when they are young; the more separated you can be from the realities of life, the better you can be at committing to such an unattainable goal as Olympic glory. And as a woman in my twenties right now, I am more separated than I can even imagine, not just from the twelve-year-old Elizabeth I so badly miss and want to replicate in my day-to-day training, but from anyone I will have to compete against if I ever do manage this comeback.

Unfortunately, being an athlete is more physical than it is anything else. And I came back to skating not just a completely different person mentally and emotionally, but physically as well. I had grown about six inches and gained over thirty pounds since I last even attempted to skate. I was no longer training as a girl, but as a woman. And unfortunately, with that came more problems than

I was prepared to deal with. Yes, catcalling had become routine for me, but I had no idea how much worse it could get. Should I blame some of my emotions on my own insecurities? Probably. But there was so much out of my control and so much I genuinely never imagined that I would be dealing with. I don't know who would have been able to react differently. Within a few months of coming back to skating, I was dressing in oversized hoodies and sweatpants—clothing so large and loose that many moves were almost impossible to do. But it was clothing that I thought would help discourage people from talking about me. I was regularly sexually harassed by staff at the rink. At one point, I even had to change my phone number because of the threats and calls I was receiving. Eventually I became so uncomfortable with being at the rink at all that I would plan my training schedule based on which staff members were working at the rink and when.

Worse than that, I was targeted by an older male coach for no reason at all. What started with comments about my body turned into comments about my skating. One day, this man would insult my jumps, and the next, he was screaming across the entire lobby asking me about my period. On one occasion he told me which modeling photos of mine he liked to pleasure himself to. He would constantly comment on my skating, my clothing, or things he assumed about my personal life. I was often afraid to be near him, terrified that somebody would overhear his comments and think they could be in any way encouraged by me. As uncomfortable as this made me, it only got worse when two female coaches overheard one of his comments to me, followed by me bawling my eyes out in the bathroom, and felt the need to report it. I then had to detail the incidents of the last few months to a stranger while he looked at me with confusion and disgust. Afterward, I learned that no action would be taken anyway. The coach would barely get a slap on the wrist, and I would be forced to continue on, with the entire rink knowing what had happened and with rumors about me being spread by this coach and his "allies." This continues to this day. The things I have heard him say about me and others have been beyond disgusting, but I have to continue seeing him regularly, sometimes skating within feet of him, knowing the rumors that he is spreading about me and my skating—all because he thinks that I complained about him and tried to "ruin his career"—and remembering the despicable things I had to listen to for months before that. It has been awful. Some days I try to plan my schedule around him, knowing that my anxiety is only heightened when he is around, and some days making it impossible to skate at all.

He is not allowed to speak to me, which is somehow supposed to make for a less awkward and appalling situation. And worst of all, he knows me. He knows the anxiety I have struggled with and the issues I have dealt with in my skating, and he uses them against me. I have to regularly share the ice with this person who not only discussed me in perverse ways to my face and to others, but thinks it is okay after all of that to stand in my way during a practice or to stare me down as I enter a jump I am already afraid of. They say what doesn't kill you makes you stronger, but I never thought that it would take this particular kind of strength to try and make this comeback.

9

As I've mentioned, there were clearly times in my life where I felt absolutely terrified. I've had moments that I wouldn't wish upon my worst enemy. But strangely enough, none of them can compare to the fear I felt when Donald Trump announced that he was running for president. There wasn't a person in the fashion world that didn't have an opinion on Trump, 99 percent of which were extremely negative. And everywhere I went, somebody wanted to find out where I stood on every single issue. It was as if they wanted to make sure I didn't have even a hint of "Trump supporter" in me. Everywhere I went, I was told that Trump supporters were racist monsters and was confronted about my political views. And despite my house being completely covered in Trump 2016 stickers and the hopes that I had for his campaign, I never said a word. I knew what would happen to my modeling career, and I didn't want to lose the one thing that made me feel good about where I was in my life.

Coming back to skating was supposed to be an incredible feeling, and on some occasions it was! There were moments where I would skate around and remind myself of everything I had fought through to get to this point. Those moments were incredible. But the other 90 percent of the time I was incredibly discouraged and down. I had spent so many years dreaming of my comeback to skating that I often let my mind wander off much further than I should have. I imagined myself doing jumps and spins that I used to do, as if no time had passed and my injuries didn't affect me. Some days I sat and daydreamed for hours as if it would somehow make my thoughts a reality. But finally stepping onto the ice proved anything but that. Skating was difficult and painful and certainly not the magical fairytale I hoped it would be inside my head. And although I was incredibly proud of myself for giving up everything to attempt this comeback, there were many days where I was left completely distraught about my chances of a future in the sport and very confused about my decision to attempt this comeback in the first place.

I had left Wilhelmina Models and found a new agency. And though it did have its fair share of flaws and people I wouldn't recommend anyone spending time with, I met some pretty cool people working there who made me feel a lot more at peace with my situation. I also had a manager I really liked and actually trusted. My time on the ice was so difficult, I tried desperately to use modeling to keep myself distracted from everything going on there. I am easily distracted, especially when it comes to work and new ideas that I have, and I knew if I focused on my modeling career, I could manage to keep all of the physical and emotional pain out of my head. My plans for college had shifted since I had gone back to training. Any ideas that I had had about being a normal college student had quickly gone out the window (not that I ever imagined myself being a normal college student deep down anyway). I applied to the Harvard Extension School in order to get my degree online from Harvard University. And let me just add right here that, despite whatever the media has decided to write about me and the lies they have chosen to spew, I did have to apply to the Harvard Extension School. Yes, anyone can sign up for classes online, but to be accepted to the degree program, you must go through an application process like you would for a regular school, take a minimum of three classes and receive a B in each. (I just had to get that out there so the media knows that you can't blatantly lie about every aspect of a random person's life just because you don't like who is in the Oval Office.) I was also going through my incredibly combative relationship. And although it was not affecting me as terribly as it once had, it was still one of the worst decisions of my life. So, all in all, was life as terrible as it could be? Absolutely not. But I wasn't in a great spot and was still in what I call my "suicidal phase," which lasted from about sixteen to twenty-one.

I've been extremely patriotic since I was a child. My parents always like to tell the story of how I ran up to the microphone during a first-grade school play right after 9/11 and screamed "I'm so proud to be an American" out of nowhere. Everybody I know makes tremendous fun of me whenever the national anthem plays because no matter why it is playing and what is going on around us, I *will* start crying. It's who I am; America is a part of me, it's as simple as that. It's something I have always known and felt and something that has only ever gotten stronger. My parents and grandparents are immigrants. Both sides of my family arrived here with little to no money or security. All that they brought with them was the hope that they would be able to live the American dream. I know what my parents and grandparents went through to get here. The struggles that they faced have stayed with me almost as if I had been there with them, every step of the way. They weigh on my shoulders with every decision that I make. I know how lucky I am to have been born in the single greatest country in the world, and I don't like having to hide that.

But despite all of the patriotism that I felt in my heart and soul growing up, when Donald Trump ran for president, that patriotism somehow got even stronger. Yes, I wanted him to win, but it was so much more than that. In a way, I saw myself in him. Yes, that sounds crazy, but hear me out. My entire life I had been told that I couldn't do this or couldn't do that. I had been bullied by teachers, friends, coaches, and family members who didn't like certain decisions I had made. I was surrounded by people who didn't want me to be myself; for some reason they preferred that I do what everyone else was doing and conform. It didn't matter if everyone else around me was doing something questionable or even wrong. And it didn't matter if what I wanted would make me happy and not cause harm to anybody. All that mattered was that I wasn't trying to be like everyone else, and people hated that.

In every group, or even industry, that I have ever been a part of, there has been a standard way of doing something and a very intense stigma around the idea of challenging that. When I chose to not follow around the other girls in sixth grade and kiss different boys, I was bullied for being "weird." When I chose to skate, I was laughed at and told I was too old to start. I was told that everyone who came before me had started younger than six years old, and I had no chance to catch up to the other skaters my age. When I chose to be homeschooled, my own family members told my parents that they were making a mistake and that I should pursue a more standard education. When I chose to model, I was told that I had to change my beliefs and my idea of sexuality in order to succeed.

No matter what I considered doing, I had a reason for it. But no matter the reason, someone was always trying to tell me "no." Why? Because it had never been done before, and that makes people uncomfortable. People like to be sheep. They like to know that they can hide in a pack and never be seen as different. Ironically, however, when you start being recognized for being different, they suddenly become very angry with you and jealous at the idea that you're being rewarded for that difference. And unfortunately, this happens with coworkers, peers, friends, and even family. My dad used to tell me that whenever anything good happened, I should only reveal it to a very select and small group of people. He always warned me about how ugly people's bitterness and jealousy can be. And despite my mom's constant fights with him about being too cynical and my obsession with proving him wrong, my life has been twenty-four straight years of him being proven right.

People are very strange. They want special attention, but they don't want to have to do anything difficult or think outside of the box in order to get it. And at the same time, they always want to make sure that you never do either of those things yourself, because then—God forbid—you would be the one who gets the special attention! It's a constant cycle of boredom and satisfactory achievements, two things that I have zero interest in. And despite it being pretty difficult to be labeled as a weirdo when I was younger, after seeing my own (once supportive) family members try and insult me as such, it eventually became a huge compliment. I love to think for myself. I like to accomplish things and I even like to fail at things, because they are usually things that most people would never have had the guts to try in the first place.

Slowly but surely, I think you guys are getting the picture. Donald Trump was cool. It's as simple as that. Most of the world didn't even know where he stood on most policies yet, but they were already infatuated with him. Was it because of the things he was saying? No! It was because he was the only one on the damn stage who was saying anything at all. Let's be honest, politics can be really dull. I've been obsessed with politics since I was a little girl, yet I still often find myself bored listening to politicians drag on and on about things that they themselves clearly don't care about. Despite what many in the media think, Americans are not stupid. We know when we are being lied to. We know when someone is speaking for his or herself and when someone is constantly relying on campaign aides to form the sentences and thoughts that come out of their mouth. I was ready for Donald Trump, but more importantly, so was America.

I want to add that this was not a political decision, but a personal one. So many people around me feel comfortable aligning with a certain political party or label. Some as young as middle school! And though I myself was guilty of that same mistake, again, I had learned from my brilliant father that that is the opposite of what we should be doing or encouraging for young people today. There is so much that all of us will learn in our lifetimes. There are so many different people that we will meet and different things we will experience; it is impossible to align completely with a political party as a teenager and know for sure that you will stick with that party forever. As a young girl, I thought that I had done enough research and decided that I was going to be a Republican forever. Unfortunately, life is never that simple. Luckily, we live in the United States of America, where we get to elect politicians for no reason at all except the fact that they appeal to us. I knew where I stood on many social issues and mostly leaned conservative. However, I also knew that there were many Republican candidates I would not have supported, and certainly never considered working for. This didn't come down to a political party for me, this came down to one person: Donald Trump.

I have to say this because he'll never forgive me if I don't: my brother knew before 99 percent of the world. He told my parents and me that Donald Trump was going to be our forty-fifth president before he had even announced that he was going to run. I had never doubted my brother before—I have no reason to, as he is one of the brightest people to ever live. But I can't say I had complete faith in his prediction. I do have to say, however, that it is 100 percent because of him that I got behind Donald Trump when he entered the race. Would I have eventually been a Trump supporter either way? Definitely. But when he first entered the race, there was a lot I didn't know about him. Luckily, my brother had done more real research on him in the month before he announced than all the "reporters" have done since then, and he assured me that he was the best person for the job. This may seem naïve, but it is the honest truth for me. No matter what anybody in the world says about somebody's character, I will always trust my brother. My brother is hands down the greatest person one could ever meet. He is simply the kindest and smartest there is, and if he was behind Donald Trump, it didn't matter what anybody else was ever going to tell me.

We lived very close to Trump Tower, so as soon as we found out that they had a volunteer center, we set out to volunteer on our first political campaign. After about ten minutes of questioning and filling out paperwork, we were phone banking for Donald Trump. A few hours later, we sat with our parents at a café recounting our day. I don't think we had been that excited in years. We were finally, even in the tiniest of ways, a part of something bigger than ourselves, and it felt amazing. This was what we thought was best for America, and I was proud of us for taking the first step in fighting for that. I may have just been making phone calls, but even just sitting there in Trump Tower and knowing that I was doing something that could help change the future of the country that I loved more than anything in the world was a huge honor.

For us, this wasn't about a political party or ideology of any kind. This was about feeling in our guts that something was right

Elizabeth Pipko

for the future of the United States and getting behind it 100 percent. Both of us are (and always have been) incredibly patriotic, and it meant a lot to us that Donald Trump brought that out in us even more and made us feel honored to be Americans with every speech he gave. And to know that we were now a teeny, tiny piece of the effort to make him president was an honor I cannot begin to describe. Again, not because it was just Donald Trump, but because it was all for the United States of America.

The jokes about Trump's campaign didn't stop. And for a man who seemed to have the entire world against him, all convinced that he had no future in the race, he was gaining in the polls practically by the hour. He was courageous beyond belief, yet also the biggest underdog for the presidency that the U.S. had ever seen. He was inspiring, every single day. And not because of the words that he was saying, but because he was getting up every single day and saying them despite the entire world being against him.

My brother and I were phone bank operators and we loved that, but I wanted more. My parents raised me to live according to my own crazy rules and dreams, and I think that is something I have always been good at. I love going after things that people think I could never accomplish. Like I said, I've been this way for quite some time. But nothing can inspire you to want to do more quite like watching a man campaign so confidently for one of the most powerful positions in the world while everybody mocks him.

Trump wasn't fielding these attacks from just one side either, he was getting them from the entire world. He watched as people on every side of the political aisle went after him and his chances of winning every single day, and he didn't bat an eye. Watching him was like watching the final scene from *Miracle*, my favorite movie. In fact, his campaign and the genuine momentum and support that he had gave me the kind of strength and inspiration I had only ever experienced from television and movies.

I desperately wanted to get more involved in the campaign. Never in my life have I been satisfied with not reaching my full potential or not shooting for the stars, no matter the activity. The 2016 Trump campaign was going to be no different. I wasn't satisfied just being a volunteer; I wanted more, and I knew exactly what I had to do. I sat for three days and wrote down everything that I thought needed fixing in the volunteer center. I discussed some plans I thought could help the campaign and things I thought they could be doing in order to get more votes. Now remember, I was just twenty-one years old at the time. I had no college degree and no real experience, just balls. And if my skating had taught me anything, it was that sometimes balls are really all you need. I knew that my best chance to get this letter to the right people would be to find a campaign intern who could bring it upstairs to the campaign office for me. After begging an intern I knew to bring my letter to the director of the data team,

I said a prayer and waited. I wasn't expecting anything but was certainly hoping for it. I hadn't felt what I used to feel on the ice in years. And if anything brought me close to that feeling, it was being in Trump Tower and being a little part of a presidential campaign.

The data director called me within twenty-four hours. The following Monday, I had my first day.

10

My time on the campaign was overwhelming. There were quite a few bumps, which I will get into, but the experience was also one that I will be eternally grateful for. This was the epitome of an experience of a lifetime. How many people in the world have worked on presidential campaigns? How many have worked on a winning presidential campaign? And how many have worked on the historic 2016 Trump campaign? Very, very few. This was an experience that taught me more in a few months than I could have learned in a decade somewhere else. More importantly, it was an honor. I was working to help elect a new president for the greatest country in the entire world. And the fact that God thought I was worthy of an experience like the one that I had is something I still cannot fathom.

On my first day of work, I sat at my desk, totally enamored with everything around me. I've had a few experiences in my life that have left me starstruck, but this, by far, took the cake. I was only twenty-one, and sitting in Trump Tower, working on a presidential campaign! It was exhilarating. In my first two hours, I saw Lara Trump walk by and immediately texted my mom, freaking out. I had no idea what I was in for when I took the job, but I certainly did not expect to be regularly mingling with the top officials on the campaign. Yet here I was, in the middle of all of the action, and I was petrified. I don't think I knew where the restroom was until my third week on the job. I didn't want to run into someone important and embarrass myself, so I avoided going to the bathroom even once I did figure it out. I also avoided eating some days as I never wanted my boss to not see me at my desk and think that I was not appreciative of the opportunity that he gave me.

Over my few months on the campaign, I regularly saw Ben Carson, Governor Christie, Mayor Giuliani, and so many others. I had no idea this could ever be my life, and I just wanted everyone around me to know how grateful I was to be there. I was living life, finally, and I was so, so grateful. I hadn't felt the exhilaration that I used to get on the ice in so long, and feeling it again was an incredible gift. This wasn't about the individuals around me and whether I agreed with every policy that they had pushed or every statement that they had made in their lifetimes. No, this was about knowing that I was taking part in a tiny piece of something that would go down in American history, and it was a huge honor.

I'll be honest, my brother and I have a strange bond (strange to others! Certainly not to me). It's one of my favorite things about my life and something I pray never changes. Weirdly enough, we've even been mocked for it by family and friends, as if people would prefer if we hated each other. Simply put, my brother is my best friend. He is the person I admire most in this world and the person I have basically shared everything with. We are only two years apart and very often get confused for twins because of how similarly we behave. He also was the reason that I ended up on the campaign. He was the person who introduced me to the idea of a President Trump, the person who assured me every time we were mocked for supporting him, and the person who gave me the confidence to write the letter that got me the job. I knew how much it would mean to him to be a part of the campaign and how much it would mean to me to have him by my side through everything. More importantly, I knew that he belonged there, much more than I did. If there was a chance that in a few months there would be a President Trump, there was nobody in the world more deserving or capable of being a part of it than my then eighteen-year-old brother. So, I made sure that, by my second day, my boss knew he needed my brother to complete his team. Anytime it was brought up that they were still looking to fill positions, I brought up my brother's name. I knew that if they gave him a chance and met him for just five minutes, they would know that they needed him. I just had to get him in the door.

I like to live my life by the phrase, "Where there is a will, there is a way." This was a perfect example of that. My brother belonged on the 2016 campaign; I felt it in my heart. I knew how much it would mean to him and how much he deserved it, and I set out to make it happen. Were there a few setbacks in my plan? As always, yes! But within two weeks, he was right by my side. I think he may have been one of the youngest, if not the youngest, staffer on that campaign, an honor I know that he takes extremely seriously. And again, another gift from God. My brother means the world to me. I had never in my life experienced anything meaningful without him by my side, and there was no chance in hell that I was going to let the 2016 Donald J. Trump for President campaign be the first.

I'm told the campaign was anything but traditional. This was my only campaign experience, and without speaking to others in politics, I probably would have never learned how different it was from campaigns before it. Our campaign was assembled by dreamers. What else can you call a group of people who are told every day that they are not only wrong in their choice of candidate but are bad people for supporting him, and yet get up and work their butts off every single day? People are surprised when I tell them just how many young people were actually involved. Not only was this a campaign going against the Clinton machine, but this was a campaign that did not have the full support of those in the GOP. We were on our own, with nothing but our hearts in the game.

We all had heart, but with just heart, you can only get so far. The work ethic of everybody on the campaign was incredible. I saw so many people who regularly left me wondering if they were even going to make it till Election Day. Some would work until 3 a.m., fall asleep at the office and wake up two hours later just to begin working again. The commitment that these people had, not for their jobs, but for their country, was incredible. I remember especially being impressed with Kellyanne Conway. My desk was right outside the studio where many of the top staffers on the campaign filmed their TV segments. The level of commitment that she brought to the job was something that I genuinely had never seen before. I often remember her running back and forth to the studio to film her third or fourth segments of the day; she had been working and standing in her heels for over fifteen hours straight already and had no signs of stopping. She was not only an incredibly hard worker, something that should be respected no matter what side of the political aisle you fall on, but she also ended up being the first successful female campaign manager in our history, an accomplishment that should be celebrated by both political parties. And to be a fly on the wall as she literally changed the course of American history showed me just how hard one has to work in order to accomplish anything worthwhile. It was an extremely important reminder that I certainly needed.

Be prepared, because I plan to mention this often. Many in politics are corrupt, something I will talk more about later on, but something I'm sure most of you reading this are well aware of already. When you look at politicians, usually depending on what side of the aisle you lean and where you get your news, many politicians and political operatives will be presented to you in different ways. If someone is in politics for even a year or two, there is most likely already something they have done that can be manipulated and presented in a way that looks corrupt. Some of these accusations are truer than others, but they will always exist, about everybody. My dad taught me that there is something that you can learn from everyone, and that's exactly what I set out to do on the Trump campaign and in my life. I don't care what you think of Kellyanne Conway. Whatever you are going to tell me, I have probably heard it before. I'm telling you that she proved that a woman could lead a successful presidential campaign in the United States of America, something that means a hell of a lot to me and to many other women out there. If you can't find the power in that, you are letting politics play with your mind way too much. Unless you personally know any of these politicians, political operatives, or political activists that you keep up with regularly, remember that the media's job is to frame these people in different ways, depending on what they want you to believe that day. And remember that many of these people are career politicians, and no matter how much you admire them, they most likely have something dirty in their past. Don't look to these people for moral guidance, and don't spend your days arguing with people who have different political views about whether these people are good or bad. Find something you can learn from each of them and use that to grow as a person in your own right. Politics is not a religion, and people should stop treating is as such.

One of my jobs on the campaign was to manage all of the volunteers that we had. It was a job that often left me in tears as I got to hear firsthand from regular people just how much Donald Trump running for office meant to them. I watched people change their schedules completely in order to volunteer for the campaign. A nurse told me that she requested the night shift at work so she could volunteer for the campaign during the day. Men and women of all ages came in from all over the Tri-State Area just to make some calls and do what they could for our country. It's incredibly humbling to regularly sit with elderly people who tell you how much our country means to them and how much the Trump campaign meant to them. We even had a homeless woman who came in regularly to volunteer. One day she handed us a note and a twenty-dollar bill, explaining to us that it was all she had but that she wanted it to go toward the campaign. Donald Trump meant so much to so many people. I just wish those who dislike him could understand that. He brought not just joy, but hope, to so many Americans. It was truly an honor to bear witness to that every single day, especially because there were many occasions where I found myself overwhelmed with everything going on and definitely did not have the ability to take everything in as much as I should have. Some days, I wanted a break from the intense workload, and on other days, I just needed a moment to remember why I was doing something that caused me to lose so many friends and family members. I would always go to this little room that we had in the office, which was filled completely with gifts and notes that had been sent in for Donald Trump. Some days, when I would get off of work early, no matter how exhausted I was, I would sit in that room and spend all night reading those letters. A few people even sent in their military medals and awards, wanting them instead to go to Trump. There is no group of people I respect more than our veterans, and to see what he meant to them was the most beautiful thing. These were people who had risked their lives for the future of our nation, and now all they wanted was to see a Trump presidency. I just wanted to do all that I could to help make that happen—for them and for all Americans.

I wish there was enough of an effort by the media to show the world what Donald Trump meant to so many people. Not because I think it would have been a good thing for Trump, but because I think it could have been a good thing for the country. When the media spends all their days painting candidates and their supporters as bad people (which candidates they attack obviously depends on which channel you are getting your information from), it teaches people that they are allowed to attack others as well. I never judge someone by their political affiliation or the candidate who they voted for in 2016 or any other election. I judge them for the reasons that they chose to go out and make that vote in the first place. If we all spent more time taking into account the fact that other people, even with different views, vote for the same exact reasons we do, it would get us back to a place where we could hopefully start healing as a nation. If somebody voted for Hillary Clinton in 2016 because they genuinely thought that was the best thing for our country, I respect them. None of us know what the right answers are. Many think that they do, but the truth is that nobody really does. What we know is that we love our country and vote with the hope of making it better. Deep down, many of us have a lot more in common than the media would like to allow us to believe. Those similarities should be celebrated and used to bring people together, not highlighted as differences that should keep us angry and apart.

There are so many days and nights from the campaign that stand out to me. I could write another book just about that! But

I signed an NDA, and unlike some lovely folks (you know who I'm talking about), I don't plan on breaking mine right now. But I'll tell you about the moment that was one of the most talked-about in our country, and possibly even around the world. It was October 8, and the infamous *Access Hollywood* tape had just been released. I was actually on the phone with a volunteer when it happened and was totally unaware of the chaos going on at first. I got off the phone and could immediately tell something had happened. I looked over at my co-worker. "Check the internet," he said. "What site?" I asked. "Literally anywhere on the internet" was all I needed to hear; I knew something bad had happened. I watched the video and immediately my stomach sank. Was I offended? By a tape from a reality star that was made over ten years ago and in secret? No. But who knew how America was going to react? On any normal campaign, this would have been the end. Politics is full of people who act like monsters, but surround themselves with people who swear they don't, and apparently this silly tape was somehow worse than that. I locked eyes with my brother across the room, and for a split second, I saw a bit of concern in his eyes. Who knew what America was going to do with this?

A few hours later, the campaign was back in full swing. We were on our toes knowing what was probably going on in Trump's office and the stress that everybody was under, but we continued working as normal. I sat by myself in the back of what was the original campaign office. It was a large empty floor where *The Apprentice* was once filmed. In my spot, I could see everything that was going on·with the others on my floor and could also get enough privacy to make all of my calls without having to get up. I was staring into my computer and editing a compilation video that we were creating from tapes sent in from our supporters across the country, when I looked up and saw Donald Trump. He often came downstairs to the campaign office (his office and home were upstairs in the same building) to see how things were going and to thank us for our hard work, but he had never been this close to me specifically. I was shocked to see him, especially on such a stressful day. Of course, everybody was on high alert, making sure to look like they were working very hard as he walked around the office. I looked back at my screen and continued what I was doing. A few seconds later, I looked back up and saw him walking right over to me. I stood up, quickly wiped my sweaty hands on my pants, and took a deep breath.

"What do you think of the video?" he asked me, as if my opinion mattered to him. And weirdly enough, I think that it did. This was the most human that I had ever seen him. He wasn't asking me for a strategy to fix the mess that we were in—not that I was qualified to answer that anyway. He was asking me because he wanted to know what I, as a woman, was feeling.

"I wouldn't worry about it, Mr. Trump," I told him and went on to explain why I thought the entire thing would blow over. I think it actually may have been in that moment, after our conversation ended and he walked away, that I began to realize we could win the election. I had always known that Donald Trump was not the emotionless celebrity that the media made him out to be. To see him in this light was weirdly reassuring. I saw the concern on his face. Many out there won't believe me, and that's fine, but that moment meant a lot to me. In was in that moment that I could feel what it meant to him to have genuine support from the American people. In my gut I could feel what he was feeling. The video became much more of a shock to me in that moment than earlier when I had actually watched it. Not because it bothered me in any way, but because it bothered Donald Trump, and that meant a lot.

11

It was about four-thirty in the morning, on November 8, and I was already running late. It seemed like we had been counting down to this day for the longest time, and yet when it finally arrived, I felt anything but ready. The outfit I had planned to wear was nowhere to be found, my brother was taking too long in the shower, and I hadn't remembered to pack anything to eat throughout the day—all common issues for most mornings of a twenty-one-year-old's life. Except this was anything but a normal morning.

Election Day arrived much faster than I had expected. The magnitude of all that I was a part of hadn't hit me yet, and the idea of Election Day was one I had yet to wrap my head around. Here I was, looking for my shiny gold skirt at four in the morning as I waited for my brother to finish getting ready. He was one of the youngest people on the 2016 campaign, yet one of the most confident. We passed each other a few times as we frantically got ready for one of the most important days of our lives, both secretly relieved that we would be going through it together.

My brother has a way about him. From the age of four, he has displayed a confidence and wisdom only found in a much older person. It's his demeanor and wisdom that I have learned to rely on in times of fear or concern. This was certainly one of those times. We were about to walk into Trump Tower on November 8, 2016, to put in our final day of work on a campaign that we were told was destined to lose. I believed in Donald Trump. If I hadn't, I wouldn't have put in the hours that I did. However, I would be lying if I said that I woke up confident that morning. I was scared and anxious and every emotion that you could imagine, but my brother was not. He'd wink at me with every passing glance, one headphone in his ear as he nodded along to his favorite pump-up music as if he was heading to a gym session. My brother had told me in the spring of 2015 that Donald Trump was going to run for office and that Donald Trump was going to win. And in the eighteen months since his prediction, he was laughed at and screamed at and everything in between by friends, strangers, and family members. He was ready for his vindication; and I was just glad to have him by my side.

We walked into Trump Tower by five-thirty. I was cautiously optimistic about my chances to ask my boss to let me sneak out to do the one thing I had dreamed about doing since the seventh grade. Our voting location was only a few blocks away, and I knew that if I brought him his favorite coffee order and promised to hurry, he'd grant me my wish. I hadn't realized until that day that many of my fellow staffers were not from New York City, had probably already taken care of their out-of-state voting, and would not be in the same predicament as me. I walked over to my boss and handed him his coffee; he looked back at me and said, "You have ten minutes."

By 5:53 a.m., I was standing in line with my brother at our voting location. I was going to cast my vote for the first time in my life, and I was ecstatic. While heading back to the office, I stopped at a crosswalk right next to a police officer. He took his time looking at me, gave me a long smile, and went on his way. I looked down and noticed that my coat was unbuttoned, and my Team Trump jacket was showing. I could feel a tear forming as I realized what had just happened. In that moment, it all hit me. Today, I wasn't Elizabeth Pipko; I was an American. And I wasn't voting for my future; I was voting for America's. In that moment it didn't matter that we had just witnessed one of the most vicious campaign seasons in American history. In that moment, I forgot all the terrible things that had been said about me and my family, by people we had trusted and cared about, just because we supported Donald Trump. In that moment, I didn't feel like I was part of a campaign anymore; I just felt like an American.

At around eleven-thirty in the morning, Donald Trump came in to thank us for all of our hard work. He seemed so calm and content; I couldn't understand how he was keeping it all together. It may have still been morning, but it felt like the day had long been over. The clock was moving slower than it ever had, and the answers I thought I would have by this time were nowhere to be found. The day continued on with much less action than I had expected. By two in the afternoon, I found myself sitting and texting with my mother, hoping for some kind of relief. I assumed that she would calm me down as I sat and waited for what felt like the slowest race in history to be over. Instead, I received links to bogus news articles and more hysteria than I had already created inside my own head. How could I forget that she and I were practically twins?

By two o'clock, a friend asking me to borrow hairspray became the highlight of my afternoon. Every time I picked up my phone or looked at a television, I was reminded of the fact that we could end the night in tears, and any distraction was a good one. Since my parents were only a few blocks away, and equally as erratic, I asked them to distract themselves by purchasing a can of hairspray and bringing it to Trump Tower. I came downstairs to get it and found my mother with tears in her eyes. Just a few moments earlier, Donald Trump had left the building to go vote, and as the security guards were guarding him, they asked my parents to move out of the way. "They said, 'Excuse me, folks, the president is coming through,'" my mother said to me. And I realized all at once just how real this was to her, the police officers, and so many others. Again, it hit me how lucky I am to be an American and to be a part of a day with such magnitude.

I was determined to take in every remaining moment of the day. I was in Trump Tower on Election Day, a part of one of the wildest campaigns in history, and I was beyond proud. I beg any of you reading this right now who may not have supported President Trump in 2016 to try to see where I am coming from with this. This wasn't even about being proud to support Trump. This was about a victory for a twenty-one-year-old who got to be a part of history in a major way. A victory that she never thought she would experience and one that most people would agree was an accomplishment, no matter their political leanings, before the 2016 election caused the havoc that it did.

I sat and thought about everything that had gone on in the past year, as our country dealt with a more vicious political divide than I thought I'd ever experience. I thought about the lady in my building who had seen me in a Trump T-shirt and told me, "That's so unfortunate. You really looked like a smart girl." I thought about the friends I had grown up with who called me a racist and a bad Jew for supporting Trump. I thought about the family and friends who had mocked my parents when they heard I was being homeschooled, as if it meant that I would never amount to anything respectable in my future. I thought about my uncle who took the time during a holiday celebration to come over to me and tell me how unfortunate it was that I chose to support and work for Donald Trump, the one Republican candidate who could never beat Hillary Clinton. I thought about the broken girl, who just yesterday was crying over an ankle and a boy. I got myself here, by myself, and with my own determination. I got myself onto a presidential campaign. And I was going to enjoy it.

For the first time in months, I felt a weight lift off of my shoulders. I had kept this hate with me for so long, and I was ready to let it go. Not only was I proud of myself for remaining kind to all those who had insulted me along the way, but I was proud of myself for sticking it out. I was proud of myself for sleeping an average of four hours a night as I balanced school, an athletic comeback, and working full-time on a presidential campaign. And I was proud of myself for sticking to my guns. "Donald Trump is what's best for our country," I thought to myself, and I love America way too much to not fight for what I think is best for her.

By the evening, everyone was exhausted. We had spent the day glued to our laptops and phones, and in that moment, everyone was probably just relieved to know that there was nothing left for us to do. It was in America's hands now. At around eight-thirty, I was getting tired of the texts from my parents, asking me for answers I didn't have. And I was tired of avoiding my laptop for fear of looking at results besides the ones I was supposed to be tracking. I looked at what had come in already for Florida and saw much more red than I had expected. The lawyer I was working with quickly looked up the results from Florida in 2012, and we began to compare. In that moment, Kellyanne Conway walked by and bent down to look at what we were doing. She put her hand on my back as I enthusiastically showed her just how little we needed to do to secure Florida. "If we can count on the panhandle, like we have in recent elections, we got this," I said to her. She squeezed my shoulder and walked away, almost afraid to get too excited too early on.

At nine o'clock, South Dakota was called for Donald Trump. I remember because I looked to my left and my right and realized I was standing by myself and watching the TV screen. I looked behind me and saw my brother at his laptop, focused as can be on exit polls, and a few others scattered around the room. Then, by the staircase, I heard a scream, "everyone, upstairs!" I grabbed my brother and followed the others. There, we had our campaign war room (the war room for the entire campaign cycle until election week), a giant room that the communications team was set up in during the campaign. The numbers were coming in.

In that moment, I was in a room with the Trumps, the Pences, staffers that were my friends, staffers that were anything but my friends, and others I'd never met. But it didn't matter. In that moment, all of our prayers were getting answered right in front of our eyes, and I couldn't believe it. What felt like only a few hours ago, the same people were telling me to prepare for a rough night. And here they were, screaming and crying together. The states were starting to come in: Florida, North Carolina, Michigan, all the states that we were worried about, and we were ahead. The feeling of being in that room was one of the greatest feelings of my lifetime. For a team of people that had been surrounded by so much negativity for months, this was an incredible reward.

By nine-thirty, we knew. Donald Trump had won the election. Every emotion in the world had taken over me. I was ecstatic beyond words, angry at myself for not having more faith, and grateful to God for thinking I deserved to be a part of such a moment. After squeezing my brother more times than I could count, I left the celebration to go find Darren, who I had been dating for about two weeks at that point. I went back downstairs to the war room to find him seated on the floor and clutching a bottle of water. "I think we actually won," he told me. And there I was, with the soulmate I had just met only a few weeks ago, living through one of the biggest moments in American history. I realized then that even though the numbers looked good on TV and we knew from our internal polling that we had won, America still had no idea. Seated there on the floor with the man I knew was my future, I called up my parents and told them we had made history. My dad, the most committed pessimist you could ever meet, refused to believe me. I put Darren on the phone to explain to him how we knew that we had won, only realizing after handing over the phone that this was Darren's first time interacting with his new girlfriend's father and the anxiety I had most likely caused.

By ten-thirty that evening, it was time to celebrate. I looked up from my phone and saw David Bossie screaming my way. His voice held more happiness than I had heard from anyone on our campaign in months—"Get out of here! It's time to celebrate." And we were off. I called my parents one more time and told them to get dressed for the celebration. Listening to the confusion in their voices, I realized how little faith they still had in the news I had given them. I had no idea what the news channels were saying, but I knew that we had won, and I wasn't going to let one more moment go by without reveling. Darren, being part of the political team, had to remain at Trump Tower for some last-minute polling while the rest of us headed to the Hilton Hotel. The hotel was only a few blocks away, so we decided to take everything in and walk to the celebration. Those five blocks were magical. I'm sure there were celebrations and protests going on all around me, but I saw none of that. All I saw were members of the NYPD smiling from ear to ear and police officers hugging and cheering with gratitude and bliss in their eyes. And for the third time on that incredible day, I thanked God for making me an American.

The celebrations from that night are all a blur. My only memory from the evening of November 8 was looking for Darren as he made his way into the party right before Donald Trump arrived to speak. My concern at that point shifted from winning the election to introducing the man I was in love with to my parents for the very first time—and on one of the craziest days in American history. I remember squeezing my mom's arm as he was walking over. "Be nice to this one, please. I'm crazy about him," were the only words I could muster on that incredible evening where our lives were forever changed. There I was, twenty-one years old, standing with my four favorite people in the world, about to be addressed by the president-elect of the United States of America, surrounded by chants of "USA" in the most extraordinary moment of my young life.

I'm adding this because it's extremely important to me to say. I love my country, and respect anybody else who does as well. I enjoyed being a part of the 2016 election for so many reasons, many of which most likely could not be understood by anyone who didn't experience the campaign or my life right alongside me. That doesn't mean that the experience should not be shared or that it can't be appreciated by someone on the other side of the political aisle. I love watching victories. I especially love watching a victory for anyone who was an underdog, like President Trump surely was. I often sit on YouTube and watch different moments of triumph in politics, sports, talent competitions, and so many other things.

I certainly would have taken a few days to sulk after the 2016 election if we had lost. But that doesn't mean I would have ever thought a bad word about any one of Hillary Clinton's supporters. And it doesn't mean that I wouldn't have found myself right back on YouTube in a few weeks, looking at what people were saying her victory meant to them. I didn't support her; everybody knows that. That doesn't mean it wouldn't have been an amazing victory for women to see our first female president, something I would have (eventually) rejoiced in seeing, and something I still hope to see in my lifetime.

Most people know that I lean to the right on a lot of issues and certainly would not consider myself to align with many on the progressive left. For example, I don't agree with congresswoman Alexandria Ocasio-Cortez on most issues, but that doesn't mean that I don't admire her for all that she has done. And it definitely doesn't mean that I haven't found myself on many occasions sitting on the computer and watching her witness her own victory, full of surprise and joy that brings me to tears every time. She was an underdog in her twenties who beat out an establishment Democrat. If you are too bitter and angry to appreciate that, then

Elizabeth Pipko

I'm sorry. But there is an entire world out there, and I refuse to become someone so entangled in politics that I can't appreciate a young woman's accomplishments and what they may mean for other women or even my future daughter. And I encourage you to try and do the same. Find something about Trump's victory that you can appreciate, no matter how you feel about him. Look at the amount of people who said he couldn't do it and the way that he was mocked for his aspirations, something many of us can relate to! Or look at the patriotism and hope that he brought out in so many people, even if you don't understand why. Whatever it is that you want to see, you will always find. So, start searching for the positive, in politics, and in life; I assure you it's a much healthier and better way to live.

12

Now, I mentioned Darren in the previous chapter without giving him the introduction that he deserved. Mostly because I figured he would be angry with me if I combined our story with the story of the election, as if our story wasn't special enough to deserve its own chapter. So here it is.

As if God hasn't blessed me with enough already, it was on the Trump campaign that He gave me a gift I genuinely never expected. Being a small part of the team that won the election was one of the greatest feelings I had experienced. It felt like everything had finally come full circle for me and made everything that I had gone through up until that point completely worth it. I know that if I hadn't gotten injured, I probably would have never ended up on the campaign. I never would have been there on November 8, celebrating one of the most historic events in America's history. And I never would have met the love of my life.

I was the girl that never wanted to get married. My friends (and I) constantly joked that I would die alone because I wouldn't be able to find someone who could deal with my craziness. I also hated the idea of a lifelong commitment to someone, always thinking that I would never find a man who compared to my dad or brother. I even went so far as to tell people that I would never have kids, thinking there probably was not a person on earth that I would even consider having children with. It didn't help that I had been treated like pond scum by so many guys up until that point. I had been called every name in the book by different guys because I told them I didn't want to sleep with them. I had been cheated on, lied to, and verbally assaulted by almost everybody that I ever went out with. I had been a target of sexual harassment more times than I could count and even had to fight my way out of a trauma- tizing sexual assault on two occasions. So, let's just say, I didn't have the fondest thoughts about men and certainly had more than enough reason to think I'd never consider getting married. But as I always say, "Man makes plans, and God laughs." I like to imagine God laughing at me every time I made a comment about marriage, as I so often did, just waiting for me to turn into a puddle of goo the minute I met the man who He had created for me.

I don't say "created for me" very lightly, by the way. I'm weird in every sense of the word. And more than that, I can be incredib- ly negative, sensitive, cynical, emotional, sarcastic, bitter, and so much more. There is no doubt in my mind that God knew exactly what He was doing when He created both me and Darren; it would be otherwise impossible for somebody to understand me at the level that I thought only my brother could, or to complete me in a way that I thought nobody ever would. But that's Darren. He is everything I have ever wanted and needed mixed into one absolutely perfect person. And ironically, even as the girl who thought she would die alone, I knew the minute I saw him that he was the one for me.

Never did I think growing up that it would be on the Donald J. Trump for President campaign that I would find my soulmate, but I absolutely did. Darren was working on the political team. He worked on the floor above me, but often came downstairs as the liaison between the political and data teams. I remember the day I saw him. He was standing with my boss and cracking jokes, the kind of sarcastic jokes that I like to make and that everybody often judges me for. He was laughing, which was already a great change to what was usually a very somber work environment. But it was the way he laughed and joked that really caught my attention. People don't understand it when I say this, but I don't care—he reminded me of my dad. And in that moment, I knew he would be mine.

My entire life, I knew that whoever I married would have to compare to the men in my life, leaving me very ready to die alone. It's a huge blessing to have the family that I have, but it makes my expectations very high for all people who I meet. Each of my grandfathers could have had their photo in a dictionary as the representation of the word *mensch*. My father is the kindest, smartest, classiest man to exist, and my brother is just a taller and cuter version of him (with a bit more hair on his head). Every person I had dated up until this point was, simply put, garbage compared to them. But for some reason, when I saw Darren, I thought of my dad. He laughed like him, he walked like him, he looked at people the way that my dad does. I hadn't even met him yet, and I already knew that I couldn't afford to lose him. That night, I told my parents that I had found the man I was going to marry. I had yet to learn his last name, but I already knew.

A few days later, my boss brought a dartboard into our office. The campaign had grown, and the entire data team was moved to a lower floor. There were a lot of us, doing very different things, and we needed the space. We took over the fifth floor, which was originally where the campaign had begun. It was a giant empty floor where *The Apprentice* had been filmed, and it was decorated from floor to ceiling with notes and gifts that people had sent in for Trump. I loved it. However, my boss thought that some of our team members may have been upset with being moved down-stairs and separated from much of the campaign, and he wanted to raise the team's morale. He brought in a dartboard and hung it in the center of the room. He asked what else we thought could be brought in, and I told him that as a thank you, I wanted to purchase something for the team myself. Crazily enough, the next day, a basketball set arrived. I knew that I was going to have to get Darren's attention at some point. And with less than two months left until Election Day, I thought that the hoop could be a great way to do it. The hoop actually ended up being a great addition to our floor. On days when the stress was really just too damn high, instead of eating lunch on our breaks, a few of us would play horse or simply shoot around. Many of the higher level staffers from upstairs often came down to let off some steam as well. And as great as the hoop was for our office and everyone around, most important to me, it got Darren's attention.

We spent about two weeks having some extremely awkward, and yet extremely deep and meaningful conversations. By the third week, we were both hooked on each other. Before I learned that he liked me, I worried about him moving back to DC and never seeing him again. I wanted him to know how much our conversations meant to me and how much his presence helped me. I'm not going to lie to anyone, the campaign was really rough. I went home in tears on many, many occasions. It was knowing that he was in the building and around to make me laugh whenever I needed that actually made some really difficult campaign days a hell of a lot easier. In the middle of September, I started a letter that I planned to send to him (thanking him for our conversations) in case we went our separate ways after Election Day. Again, God had other plans.

Darren and I went on our first date on October 27, 2016. On November 8, 2016, we won the election. On January 20, 2017, we watched Donald Trump become President Trump. On February 1, 2017, Darren moved to New York City and began working on the president's reelection campaign. On September 14, 2017, Darren asked me to marry him. And on December 26, 2018, in the president's home in Mar-a-Lago, we became husband and wife. That's my fairytale, and as my brother said in his toast on our wedding day, "Someone had to run for office and win the presidency for us to get together."

Darren is a gentleman. That's the best way to describe him. He is a man in every sense of the word. He supports me in everything I want to do, something I've never experienced. He loves me in a way I never knew a man could love me. With the loss of my grandfathers, I always thought that I would never know what it felt like to be loved unconditionally on that level again. But his love reminds me of theirs: completely unconditional. It is the one thing I don't ever have to question and the one thing that makes me stronger than I ever thought I could be. I never thought people like him even existed anymore, and I'm so beyond grateful to have him by my side for the rest of my life, all thanks to President Trump. He's another reason I will never in my life doubt God and His existence. I know someone is out there not only looking out for all of us but making better decisions for us than we ever could ourselves. I knew I belonged on that campaign before I even got there, and now I will forever know why.

While I am on the topic, I'd like to bring up my in-laws because it is important to me to point out just how incredibly lucky I feel to have them in my life. My immediate family is absolutely incredible, but I have always felt judged by both friends and other family members. Apart from my parents and brother, it always seemed like there was nobody who wanted me to be happy. Or they did, but with conditions. I was judged for every single thing that I did, very often to the point of tears. Like I said earlier, I learned as soon as I began skating and saw everyone's reactions to both my successes and failures on the ice, that my dad was right: there will be very few people in the world that genuinely want nothing but the best for you. I never thought I needed more people in my life (I'm super sensitive and hate to be disappointed by people, so I keep my circle ridiculously small), but to have them has been a huge blessing.

They are the least judgmental people in the world, and they represent exactly what I think is missing in so many people right now. They want me to love their son and for their son to love me, and they want us to be happy, that is all. They are exactly what all people should be and show me every single day how all people should treat those whom they love. When I tell them stories from my days on the ice, I know that they are listening. When I tell them about things that matter to me, I know that those things will suddenly begin to matter to them. And when I need a reminder at any point in time that God is looking out for me, I remember that He sent these wonderful people to me. I think about the fact that my future children will have the two best sets of grandparents that any children could have, and I know that everything will be okay.

Now this is something that is incredibly difficult for me to talk about. In fact, I went back and forth for quite some time, debating whether it was a topic that I wanted to include in this book. It's a part of my story, and it's something I am prepared to share with the world; however, it's something I am still probably not prepared to hear others discussing. It is perhaps one of the most sensitive experiences of my life thus far, but one I believe needs to be explained and shared as it relates to one of the most important aspects of my life—my Jewish faith.

I knew when I saw Darren that I wanted to spend my life with him. It was the clearest that my brain had ever felt. This was not a decision that I made through deep thought and consideration; it was something that I felt in my gut and couldn't fight. It was almost as if I didn't have a choice in the matter—I was supposed to be with him. But that doesn't mean that I didn't try to fight God, fate, and myself every step of the way. Why he stayed with me through that, I will never know. It was almost as if all of my hesitation and confusion was a test for him, one that he passed with flying colors.

And by sticking by my side as I dealt with everything, he only made my decision even harder. I can't even count the number of evenings we had where things would be going exceptionally well, only to end in tears because I let my thoughts and worries get the best of me. I remember when we took a trip to Florida on one occasion, and after getting ready for a movie one night that we were excited to see, we stood in my living room as I just bawled hysterically, questioning every aspect of our relationship. There were barely any words exchanged because he knew that there was nothing he could say. This was something I was going to have to accept in my heart, or we would have to separate.

My grandfather was one of my biggest inspirations. He was one of the proudest Jews that you could ever meet. He was a well-known artist back in the Soviet Union where he grew up, however he was never allowed to display the works that meant something to him. He often painted at night and in the dark, fearful that he would be caught painting art that displayed his love of Judaism and be punished. He even regularly risked his life, raising money, and helping Jews to escape the Soviet Union and flee to Israel. He came to the United States with my grandmother, aunt, and mom in 1974 when the United States was able to send wheat to the Soviet Union in exchange for Jewish refugees. He and my grandmother attended a synagogue service together for the first time that year, led by Rabbi Arthur Schneier in Park East Synagogue, the synagogue that my parents later married in and the synagogue I now call my second home.

No matter what the conversation was that was going on at the time, my grandfather managed to turn it into a talk about Judaism. Growing up, it was very clear that he made it his mission to make sure my cousins, brother, and I knew just how lucky we were to be born in the United States of America and to get the opportunity to practice our religion openly and proudly, something he had not gotten the chance to do. He often explained the importance of us marrying a fellow Jew and continuing on the legacy that so many before us fought to keep alive; leaving me completely convinced that there was no choice for me but to marry a Jew one day. It is a responsibility that we have as Jews that many others do not understand, but one I often speak about. Of course, people in other religions may feel it is important to share a faith; however, the responsibility that we have as Jewish people is a greater one. There are so few of us still around today, with many inter-marrying or abandoning the religion altogether. A simple example is me knowing that out of everybody that I went to school with—in a very orthodox school, by the way—maybe a handful still believe in keeping Shabbat or even attempt to keep kosher. Does it make them bad people? Of course not. But it makes it difficult to one day pass on the traditions I was raised on to my children, if I know that those around me don't feel the need to do the same.

And it's worrisome and sad for those, like my grandfather, who fought for us to be here in the United States and to be able to practice our religion without fear of being caught.

So many young people today have forgotten what our ancestors fought to keep alive, making it very difficult for us to continue on and to prosper as a people. For me, there was never a question—if I was going to ever get married, it would be to a Jewish man who would raise a family that understood what it meant to be a Jew. My grandfather passed away a famous artist, having worked with the likes of Elie Wiesel and Dizzy Gillespie, to name a few. But much more important to his legacy was his dedication to the Jewish faith—something I vowed to myself I would also try to live up to, when he passed away in 2017.

My grandfather suffered from terrible Alzheimer's for the last five years of his life. It was one of the most difficult things that our family has had to go through. His wisdom was something that surrounded me growing up, and something I very naively didn't know I would need until it was too late. I remember when he was first diagnosed, the first thing to go was his short-term memory. When I told him about how I was coming back to skating and had gotten Israeli citizenship in the hopes of one day representing our people on the world stage, he held my hand and cried. It was one of my favorite moments with him. And because of his Alzheimer's, I got to experience that moment with him more than ten times.

He never remembered what I had originally told him, with each conversation going the same way and ending in hugs and tears. Making him proud was one of my favorite feelings in the world. Unfortunately, with that also came my terrible fear of ever disappointing him.

When I met Darren, I knew I was supposed to marry him. At the same time, I knew that he wasn't Jewish. Clearly you can understand my confusion. I was absolutely petrified. I knew that we were in love. More importantly, I knew that he was in love, and the last thing I ever wanted to do was to hurt him. I brought the topic of religion up almost right away. I knew that letting it hang over my head and panicking in secret would not be the right way to approach anything as serious as this. In fact, when we first spoke and had no intentions of having a romantic relationship, I mentioned to him that I would never be able to marry a non-Jew. This was something I assumed would repel him, like it had other men in the past. Some days I wondered if he had even heard me clearly when I said it, because in the beginning of our relationship, when things were clearly going better than any other relationship either of us had ever had, he seemed confident and secure, never even bringing it up.

I had never loved or respected anyone like I did him and knowing that he was in a predicament this big because of me left me feeling terrible. After a few weeks of dating, I got the courage to finally bring it up on the phone. His first response was, "I can convert. I've thought about this." This was a huge surprise to me —not because he was willing to convert, as I just assumed he had no idea what that would actually entail, but because he had actually taken the time to think about it and was completely unfazed by me bringing up the topic.

What followed were weeks of confusion, as I worried about how to bring up the conversion again. I had been skeptical about conversion all my life, with many in the Jewish community to this day saying that they questioned it. I often thought about a woman I had met at my synagogue when I was seventeen who told me and a friend that I was standing with that she had converted. After asking her in which synagogue and with whom and hearing her respond with the name of a reform synagogue, my friend shockingly responded, "that's not a real conversion" and walked away. An even bigger issue for me was the fact that I had never personally believed in conversion up until that point. Maybe it was because I hadn't met many people who had converted and seen their approach and commitment to Judaism. Or maybe it was because I had seen so many people who I had known from school or synagogue who not only didn't feel that they needed to observe our customs, but laughed at me when I attempted to encourage them to try. Or maybe it was because I was taught that a Jewish soul is something that can only be created by God. Most importantly, though, I didn't have my grandpa to go and speak to.

And without his guidance and his blessing, I didn't know if I could marry anyone, let alone in a situation like this.

Before I could speak with any friends or family about this, I went to my rabbi's wife. I needed somebody's guidance and had no idea where to turn. My mother had been crying herself to sleep, which left me more upset, more confused, and more angry that I was doing this to so many people. I tried breaking up with Darren multiple times. By "tried," I mean I tried wrapping my head around the idea of breaking up with him but couldn't register it even in my imagination. I didn't want to lose him, but my religion and the legacy that my family had built was all that I had. It was what gave me the confidence to stand up to so many who laughed at me for wanting to keep kosher or to observe the Shabbat. It was what kept me strong in the face of any adversity. I knew that if my family could fight to keep their religion sacred back in the Soviet Union for so many years, there was nothing that I could not do. It was the only thing that kept me strong after my injury. As a teenager who felt like she had lost everything, I soon learned my faith was the one thing that would be with me forever and I committed to becoming more and more observant from that point on. Simply put, Judaism is everything to me, and I knew it was the one thing I would never sacrifice.

If I was going to mess up my own life, it would be one thing, but I had what felt like the weight of the entire world on my shoulders. Between my synagogue and community and all that it would mean to disappoint them and the idea of possibly hurting my parents and my grandfather, I was losing it. At the same time, I also had another person whose heart was relying solely on my decision, a situation I simply could not handle.

And while all of this was going on, without my knowledge, Darren was taking his conversion extremely seriously. Many say that I should be grateful that a man was even willing to change his religion, let alone to change his entire life. But this was the most important thing in my life. Judaism was and is what keeps my life together, and I was not going to take this decision lightly. When Darren told me that he had secretly reached out to rabbis for advice, I was shocked. Again, he is a gentleman, and when he says something he means it, something I still hadn't learned up until that point. Darren had watched documentaries that he said gave him a better idea of what Judaism meant to me and so many others. He also began studying Hebrew and different Torah portions weekly, as well as keeping a kosher diet. He was less than a year into the mere idea of being a Jew and was already more committed than many that I had grown up with. Was I less emotional and confused? Probably not. But I was hopeful. If I genuinely believed that God had sent Darren to me, how could I not believe that this was something that He wanted? Darren has one of the best souls God ever created. He has the heart of an angel and a soul that I know was blessed by God, but was that enough?

The rabbis who I had grown up with, learned from, and trusted were all that I had. I needed them to tell me the path to take and to give me their blessing. I knew that without that, marrying Darren was something that I wouldn't have been able to do. And the guilt of knowing that he had his heart set on marrying me at the same time that I was having all of these concerns was killing me. I hate to say it, but there were four evenings where I fought with my parents so much that I ended up sitting on the floor of my bathroom, cutting my arms again. I couldn't bear the pain that I was causing my parents, myself, Darren, and everyone around me. It made something that was supposed to be a beautiful time in our young lives extremely miserable and dark.

While Darren was studying day and night, I was praying. I needed an answer and had no clue where to turn to get one. We had been turned down by rabbis multiple times, each time proving more difficult to handle than the last, and we were running out of hope. The Torah says that when someone begins the process of wanting to convert, it is up to the rabbi to reject him three times in order to test his willingness to continue on. I was more than aware of this, and yet every time shocked and hurt me more than the last. I felt so much guilt for knowing what Darren was going through, but at the same time, I was falling more and more in love with him while watching his commitment to a faith that I loved so much. Darren made me proud to be a Jew. Everything that I had loved about my religion was now something I got to share with the person I had loved more than anybody I had met before. We had regular conversations about Torah portions, as well as many of our laws and traditions. Darren even bought a few Hebrew language workbooks that we slowly worked through every other day. Some days he would call me from work with questions as he sat during his lunch break and studied.

I was so moved by his commitment to understand Judaism that it actually made me love it more. I had dated Jewish men in the past, and many of them had mocked me for my obsession with staying true to the traditions and rules given to us by God. To see someone who was not born into our faith learn to appreciate it at the level that Darren had was one of the most moving experiences that I had ever been through. I remember looking over at him from the women's section of my synagogue during Shabbat services one day as he was praying. Our rabbi told him that during the conversion process it was important for him to begin to live as a Jew and to do all of the things that he would do if he were to get to convert. And not only did Darren observe every holiday and tradition, but in the two years that he was studying for his conversion, he rarely missed a Shabbat morning service. He was there every Saturday morning, praying with men who had been born into the religion and yet, had not studied it as much as he did. I loved to sit in a spot where I was able to look over at him from the women's section.

He was often surrounded by men who were dozing off (Shabbat services begin early on Saturday morning and last a few hours), and others who clearly wanted nothing to do with even attempting to understand the prayers being sung in a language they didn't fully understand. And then there was Darren. It was clear how hard he had studied by his knowledge of the words he was reading, but to see his commitment for hours every Saturday in a place that must have felt extremely unfamiliar to him was so heartwarming. I remember as we were walking out one day he pointed to a little boy and asked me "are the *tzitzit* allowed to be tucked in if they are playing a sport?" (Tzitzit are knotted fringes or tassels that you see being worn by observant Jews.)

"What?" I asked, extremely confused by the question.

"Our son, one day. If he wants to play soccer or something, are we allowed to tuck in his tzitzit so that he doesn't trip or ruin them?"

And that was when I knew.

I dreamed that one day my kids would get to grow up more religious than me, exactly like I had, bringing joy to my parents every time I told them what I had learned in Hebrew class that day. I dreamed that I would look at my future son or daughter, praying in a synagogue, as free and as proud as could be, with my grandfather looking down and knowing that all of his sacrifices weren't in vain. I knew, in that moment, that Darren could give me that dream. And even better, with everything that he had gone through, he could show our future children not just what it meant to be born Jewish, but to be able to observe the religion the way that it was meant to be observed.

Rabbi Arthur Schneier brought my grandparents to his synagogue over forty years ago when they first arrived in America. After that, he married my parents there and gave me my home away from home. I attended Rabbi Arthur Schneier Park East Day School, the school that was connected to the synagogue, from the age of three. There, I learned everything that there was to know about what it meant to be a Jew. Rabbi Schneier is extremely well known, but more important, he is extremely knowledgeable. He takes conversion as seriously as one can; I believe he has overseen less than five conversions in his sixty-plus years as a rabbi. Knowing everything that I knew about conversions, specifically in orthodox synagogues like mine, didn't help with my confidence when I brought Darren to Rabbi Schneier for the first time. Nor did it help with the pain my heart was feeling as I prayed for his approval. Rabbi Schneier felt like the closest thing that I had to a grandfather at that point. After my grandfather passed away in 2017, I turned to Rabbi Schneier for the guidance that I needed to move forward in my relationship with Darren.

I sat in a room with Rabbi Schneier for the sixth time, two years after Darren had first begun studying with the rabbis who he had been assigned to. He told me that he believed in Darren and his genuine commitment—not just to Judaism, but to me. It was the first time after speaking to many, many rabbis that we were hearing anything positive about our situation. It seemed in that moment that Darren had finally been able to convince them, as he had convinced me, of his unwavering devotion to Judaism. I believe that Hashem handpicked Darren for me. I also now believe that Hashem handpicked Darren to be a Jew, something I also often hear from many who meet him. I looked at all of the rabbis in the room that day and waited for the affirmation that I had spent over two years searching for. My heart had been in pain for over six hundred days; all I needed at this point was an answer. The process had been so beautiful, difficult, painful, emotional, and overwhelming all at the same time, and I just wanted everything to finally be okay. Rabbi Schneier looked over at Darren and told him that he believed that he was ready. I could feel my heart in my throat. After everything that we had been through, all of the rabbis that once questioned both me and Darren agreed that his devotion to Judaism was genuine and his conversion was approved to move into the final stage. I looked up, taking in everything that was going on around me, and then back at Rabbi Schneier. After what felt like a million years, I finally heard the sentence I didn't even realize I was waiting for.

"I think your grandfather would be incredibly proud."

13

When my dad came to the United States with my aunt and grandmother over thirty years ago, he said goodbye to his father for the last time. My grandfather was banned from leaving the Soviet Union and had to part with my dad not knowing if they would ever meet again. After years and years of saving up money in order to travel to Europe and see his father again, my grandfather was robbed of his visa (by the government) and suffered his third (and fatal) heart attack. It was the idea that he might never see his son again that took his life. And though I may have never gotten to meet him, I strangely enough feel more of a connection to him than I do to most others in my family. My brother was named Gabriel after my grandfather, and without ever even knowing him, I see his characteristics in my brother's being. My brother is an angel. There aren't others like him around, and I know his delicate nature and kind heart are both a continuation of my grandfather. I'm often told how much I look like him, something that makes me immeasurably happy in a way I still cannot put into words. I am often asked why I did not change my last name after marriage, and the answer is my grandfather. The name "Pipko," which I think is already adorable and extremely unique on its own, takes on a whole different meaning when I think about him. I love my husband's last name, and I'm excited for it to one day be the name of my children, but the thought of ever giving up my last name was one I could never even consider. My grandfather and I would have been best friends; that's something I'm positive about despite never having met him. And the connection I have to him is one I proudly carry with me everywhere that I go. I love my name, and I love the feeling I get when I accomplish anything large or small, knowing that it was a victory I had as a Pipko and a victory that he and I had together.

Growing up, I could always see it in my dad's eyes. With every accomplishment or special moment in our lives, even the simple ones, it was written all over his face. My grandfather wasn't there to experience us growing up, and my father could only hope that he could see everything that we had become. It felt like I had a duty to include him in everything that I was doing, even though I physically could not. At just nine years old, sitting on my father's lap after finishing a movie, he said, "I just wish he were here to see you." It broke my heart, as always, that I couldn't prove to my dad just how much I loved my grandfather and how often I think about him, even though I hadn't met him. I made him a promise that day: if I were to ever get married, I would make sure to do it on December 26, my grandfather's birthday, to make sure that he was a part of the celebration. And on December 26, 2018, I made good on that promise, making my wedding day even more special that I could ever have imagined it being.

Everything leading up to the wedding was another blur. I was consumed with confusion over Darren's conversion and what I was next going to do with my life. It never felt like I was enjoying the wedding planning as much as I was enjoying the idea of it all being over. But even then, I didn't know where my life was going to go. I had no idea what was next for me, and I wanted to make sure that marriage was not it. I wanted to be married because I was in love. As soon as my grandfather passed away, I knew that I wanted to get married as soon as possible. The idea of losing even one more person who meant something to me and not having them at my wedding one day was devastating. I knew how much any of my grandfathers would have loved to dance with me at my wedding and knowing that it wouldn't be possible already put a serious damper on things. Above all, people were incredibly nasty. Everywhere I went, friends and strangers felt the need to tell me that they thought I was too young to be married. As if their opinion mattered or there was a right or wrong age to be in love. Again, as I had already learned earlier in life, everybody has an opinion and a judgment about everything. Friends of my parents even told people I was pregnant, as that would obviously be the only reason for two consenting adults in their twenties to decide to get married. It wasn't pleasant, and to be honest, I was pretty sick of it. Darren and I wanted a wedding because we knew that it would mean a lot to our parents and we knew that the memory was something we would have forever. But deep down, all we wanted to do was run away.

My time on the campaign had brought me back to a feeling I had only ever felt on the ice. I felt a sense of purpose for the first time in a long time, and it became very addicting. I was so young and so confused by everything going on when I was injured, that despite what many people and doctors told me, I didn't realize until much later that I had fallen into a bad depression. The campaign saved me in a sense. It was almost like while I was fighting for the American future I believed in, I was also fighting for myself. I had just spent my teenage years genuinely feeling as though my life was over, and here I was experiencing something so gigantic and important that it made me feel like life was worth living again. I had every reason to be depressed and hurt, but I had no reason to give up on life and everything around me. There was so much more around me and so many people and experiences I could learn from and choose to live for, and I would have never known that if I didn't get the chance to be on that campaign. It's something I often try to explain to people when they question me for working for Donald Trump. This was such an important personal experience for me; I wish people could understand what it did for my confidence, my sense of self-worth, and my future.

As soon as it was over, all I wanted was to feel it again. My days were being spent in tears on the ice, working through every physical and emotional roadblock that I could possibly have in my way, and all I wanted was to feel a sense of meaning again. I was taking classes, trying to begin my comeback on ice, and modeling again; but I felt anything but successful. I even self-published my second book of poetry. My first book came out when I was eighteen years old and was inspired by all of the heartache that I was feeling at the time. My second book, *About You*, was named one of the best books to read before you sleep by Arianna Huffington's *Thrive Global*. I found my book, something I was incredibly proud of, on a list of books with former President Bill Clinton's new book, and I still felt the furthest from accomplished. I knew that a piece of myself was missing and had no idea where to find it.

Every week it was something new. I would watch what was being said on the news or run into a neighbor or friend and hear them say a terrible thing about the president. As crazy as it sounds, it hurt me every single time. I knew that these attacks were meant to hurt more than just President Trump; they were meant to hurt his supporters. I don't care enough about myself to feel bad about the way that I was hurt. In fact, by that point, because of my political views, I had been called so many names and attacked by so many people whose opinions I cared about that I was completely used to it. This was not about me. This was about the thousands of Americans who I got to indirectly know from my time on the campaign and my genuine faith in the fact that they were good people. I wanted to defend the Americans who felt strength and hope just from Trump's campaign. I wanted their feelings and thoughts to be explained and defended so that the country could learn something from what happened on Election Day, instead of dividing itself more. And I wanted people to see that the country that we were turning into, one where people can freely bully each other for their political beliefs, is not the country that we want to be.

It killed me inside to not be able to defend my own morals and values. I watched myself becoming more and more afraid by the day. Afraid of those around me who would want nothing but harm for me if they ever found out where I had worked and who I had supported, and afraid for the country that was turning, right before my very eyes, into everything that it stood against. My own parents had escaped from the Soviet Union, a place where their beliefs were silenced, to come to the United States to make sure that their future children could grow up differently. Everything that America stood for was being taken away, all because people were upset that they did not see the result they wanted in the election—the result that they had been promised by every news station, prominent pollster, and politician around.

I watched as people grew angrier and angrier with each other for no reason at all. I watched as my manager stood in the office and yelled about the evil people in the White House and all that they were doing to disgrace America. I watched as friends I grew up with posted nastier and nastier things on social media, promising to target anyone who they found out had supported Donald Trump. I watched as influential celebrities across our country made threats against the president and his supporters as if they had forgotten the backbone of what makes us all Americans to begin with. I was petrified, but I knew that I could not go on this way much longer. I can't speak for everyone, only for myself, when I say I could never treat anybody the way that I have been treated by many just because they voted for Hillary Clinton in the election. I hope many will join me in saying that the wrath many Trump supporters have had to experience is insanely uncalled for and should be a lesson to us all on how not to act when we don't like something political.

Remember the famous model that I mentioned earlier? The one who I got the chance to shoot with on one of my very first jobs at Wilhelmina? Well, I ran into him again. And where of all places? The volunteer center at Trump Tower. That's right, back when I was on the campaign, one of my tasks was managing the volunteer center in the building where I had begun myself. I went downstairs one day and saw a familiar face sitting there, covering his face with a hat and making calls for then candidate Donald Trump. He begged me not to tell anyone that I had seen him there, and I assured him that his secret would, of course, be safe with me. I often think about this moment, remembering the fear in this man's eyes when he realized that somebody he knew had recognized him. This was somebody I had looked up to. And for his confidence of all things! And now he was covering his face while volunteering for a presidential campaign, something that so many got to do proudly for candidates before. It simply wasn't fair.

All I could think about was what my grandfather would tell me. Both he and Iosif taught me the same thing: to never fear anything. I've always been incredibly sensitive and anxious. In fact, it has really only gotten worse since I have gotten older, which I know would disappoint them greatly. They were never afraid of anything, and there is no way that they would have wanted me to continue on modeling while living a secret life on the side, terrified to share the views I had been so proud of up until that point and to stand up for my country, which I cherish more than almost anything else. Modeling had brought me so much joy, but this was something greater. This was not about living for myself and dealing with my own insecurities. This was about giving all of that up and living for something so much bigger. This was about the United States of America. A country that I am just so damn grateful for, a country that so many have given their lives for, and a country that deserved better than what it was getting. I bothered Darren every single night, mulling over my decision to come out with the secret that I had worked for the president of the United States in the hope of making a real change. I can't even begin to go into how crazy it is that in this day and age, that was something I had to hide, but that is our reality, and it's something certainly worth fighting against.

You might be asking yourself why I keep bringing up my modeling career? It's because I knew that if I told the world about my few months working on the Trump campaign, I would never model again. No, I wasn't world famous, but I knew that I had accomplished enough in my modeling career that my secret would attract some kind of attention, and certainly attacks. I was petrified. The bullies I had dealt with as a child still had a way of getting to me, so to think that I had to prepare myself for much more of that was something incredibly hard to wrap my head around. I wanted to do better, I wanted to be better, but I was scared to lose myself. I was terrified that someone's attacks or words would trigger something in me and take me back to the days of the anxiety that had caused me so much harm. The last thing I wanted to do was to go back to regularly vomiting, not eating, or harming myself.

A few months before my wedding, Kanye West went viral for some of his statements about Donald Trump. His support for the president certainly garnered him a lot more attention than I would ever get, something I'm sure he knew would happen, and yet he expressed himself with more confidence and poise than I could ever imagine doing. He knows this world better than most, and he knew what it would mean for his life, career, and family to out himself as a Trump supporter, and yet, he did it anyway. Why? To support others who were scared to do the same. Fear has been such a huge factor in my life. As a little girl, before I began skating or modeling, I was often anxious and fearful of many things others rarely think about. Even before I was injured, the little figure skater I talk about who had more confidence than I could ever imagine having now, feared a lot of things. And from skating to modeling to dating to just living life, that anxiety was never something that went away; in fact, it got worse and worse the older I got. I knew how controlling and crippling this fear had been in my life up until that point, and all I wanted to do was break free from it. If I gained nothing else from the experience, maybe I would at least go on fearing my jumps a little bit less.

It was on *Jimmy Kimmel Live!* where Kanye West said exactly what I needed to hear in order to make my decision. And I want to stress this means so much more than politics. This was a decision that I wanted to make so that I could think back to it for the rest of my life and know that life was not worth living with fear. This was a moment I wanted to create for myself so that I could grow up and have something to think back to and hold on to when I needed the confidence to go on. And thanks to Kanye's words, I decided to create that moment for myself. I'd like to write them for you below:

"It's funny, you know. In this world that we live in there's two main motivating forces, and I tweet about it all the time. It's love or fear. And you can't explain love. You know my cousin is locked up for murder and I love him. So, he did a bad thing, but I still love him. And just as a musician, African American, guy out in Hollywood, all these different things you know? Everyone around me tried to pick my candidate for me and then told me every time I said I liked Trump, that I couldn't say it out loud or my career would be over, I'd get kicked out of the black community because we're supposed to have a monolithic thought, we can only be Democrats. So even when I said it right before I went to the hospital and I expressed myself and when I came out I had lost my confidence, so I didn't have the confidence to take on the world and the possible backlash and it took me a year and a half to have the confidence to stand up and put on the hat no matter what the consequences were and what it represented to me is not about policies, because I'm not a politician like that, but it represented overcoming fear and doing what you felt no matter what anyone said; and saying you can't bully me, liberals can't bully me, news can't bully me, the hip-hop community can't bully me, because at that point, if I'm afraid to be me, I'm no longer Ye, that's what makes Ye. And I actually quite enjoy when people actually are mad at me about certain things."

Somehow Kanye put everything that I had been feeling, not just for the past few years, but for almost a decade, into words. Fear was controlling my life as it always had. I had to be honest with myself for the first time in three years. The only reason my skating was not progressing as I had hoped it would was not the pain in my ankle or even the fact that I had been off of the ice for years, but the crippling fear that I felt every time I stepped into the rink. I was letting fear rattle me to the point of suffering, all the while being very cognizant of the negative effect it was having on my life and my future. All I wanted was for the fear to go away. All I wanted was to free myself of the fear and anxiety that I had let rule my life up until that point and start fresh. If Kanye could do it, I was ready to do it too.

As confusing as it sounds, this was not about politics. This was about everything that I believed in. This was about the life I wanted to lead and the life I wanted to show others was possible as well. The United States means so much more to me than two political parties and the thousands of candidates we will be introduced to in our lifetimes. I knew that this fight was about the future of the United States of America. A future that could be lived freely and without any concerns or fears. A future I knew that so many young people around the country deserved. I couldn't care less who the hell you voted for. I just want you to know that you're entitled to that vote and the opinion that you have. And that you should declare it proudly no matter who it is around you that disagrees. I was ready to stand up for everything that I believed in and hopeful that if nothing else at all, I could go on with my life more courageous and confident than ever before.

The United States means so much, not just to us living here, but to others around the world. In fact, as I am writing this right now, those in Hong Kong who are protesting for their freedom are doing so by singing the United States' national anthem and waving American flags. The United States of America is the greatest country on the face of the earth. It has given me and my family more opportunities and joy than any other place on earth could, and I owe her everything that I am. If Kanye could put on his MAGA hat on national television, I knew that I could as well. This was no longer about me. It was about those who risked their lives to come here and give me the greatest life imaginable, for those around the world still waiting and dreaming of a life in the United States, and for those who fought and died for the very freedom that I was so scared to express.

I said a prayer and began my plans for 2019, knowing that my life would never be the same again.

14

Immediately after my wedding, I got to work. I never believed in half-assing anything, and this certainly was not going to be when I started. I found a publicist and laid out the plan that I had come up with. My future was completely on the line, and I knew this had to be approached correctly. There is a stigma attached to the word "model" and the last thing I wanted was to have that be a negative part of my story. This was going to be about so many things at once and I had to make sure that the narrative came across just right. I had to make sure that people understood where I was coming from as a woman and a model. I had to clearly explain the repercussions I was afraid of facing if anyone in the modeling industry found out about my political work, while also having to explain what it felt like to keep something so important to me a secret in the first place. And of course, all while expressing how absolutely insane it was that anybody had to keep their political views a secret in the United States of America at all.

As well as the extremely difficult circumstances and logis-
tics that I dealt with while hiding a huge portion of my life for
multiple months, I wanted people to understand this was something many others were going through even though they maybe
weren't in the same predicament that I was in. At the same time,
I wanted people to understand that my role on the campaign was
a serious one, and that I worked incredibly hard and was beyond
humbled and honored to have gotten the opportunity to be on the
campaign in the first place. It was a huge responsibility that I took
very seriously and wanted to make sure others would as well.

I also wanted people to understand how important America
was to me. When it comes to my upbringing and everything that
I came from, appreciating the freedoms of the United States of
America is of the utmost importance, which is a main reason for
my decision to tell this story in the first place. The freedoms that
we experience in the United States are too important, specifically
to people like my family members who had to escape in order to
finally be able to experience them, and that is something I cannot
bear to watch being taken from other people. Sure, the United
States is not and never will be anything close to the Soviet Union,
but to watch people fearing for their safety for simply admitting
who they voted for just seemed all too familiar to the stories my
parents used to tell me.

This was also, selfishly, something very personal to me. So many idiots out there decided that they could tell me what direction my life was going in because I decided at twenty-three years old to get married. I could not believe just how disrespectful and bitter people became when they heard my plans. The things that they came up with and had the nerve to say to my face were simply absurd. Women can be and do absolutely anything that they want, married or not. And my getting married meant nothing except the fact that I was in love, simple as that. It did not mean that I was suddenly going to be a housewife, at home barefoot and pregnant, before my twenty-fourth birthday. No, it actually meant the opposite, because it was with my husband's support that I felt strong enough to face the world, to stand up for all of the things that I believe in, and to embark on this new journey.

As you can clearly tell, I had a lot on my mind, and my anxiety was in full crazy mode. I told my publicist that we had two weeks to find someone to do the story. I needed to find someone who was a good writer, as well as someone trustworthy so I could confidentially share my personal story. I knew, especially with what I had seen the president and many others in politics dealing with, that any journalist can twist your words and change the meaning of anything that you say. This was a huge concern for me. I also had to convince someone from a reputable outlet to want the story in order to give it legitimacy. Like I said, this was serious to me. I knew that when involving the president's name or campaign in anything that I decided to do, I had to put in the work to make sure that it was done correctly out of respect. The office of the president is something meant to be respected, regardless of your views on the person occupying it at any given time. If Hillary Clinton had been the one elected and in office, I would have put just as much effort into respecting all involved.

Immediately, I sensed that we were having issues. I had worked with my fair share of publicists, agents, and outlets from my modeling days, and I knew exactly what it felt like when I could confidently say that something was going to get done. And after over two weeks of back and forth with different writers, my publicist was still unable to find someone at the level that I wanted. I was starting to get pretty worried and began to do my own research and planning. My entire life, people have told me how "lucky" I was to get some of the opportunities that I have had. But little do people know just how much work went into all of those opportunities. My dad always taught me that hard work was the one thing you could always count on. No matter what life throws out at you and how unpredictable everything can be, the one thing that you should always make sure of is that you worked harder than anyone else possibly could. He also taught me that no matter what life throws at you, in one way or another, it is always your fault. This publicist failed at finding me the right person to do the story. Could I blame him for that and give up? Of course. But who would really be at fault? Me. I always could have tried harder, worked more, presented the story differently, followed up more often, given more suggestions about who to approach, and so on. This was my approach when it came to modeling, schoolwork, job opportunities, and everything else. This was how I approached everything, something I doubt will ever change.

As anyone who gets anything done knows, it's best to just do it yourself; so I did. I had done two weeks of research and had a chart of different reporters organized by how friendly they were to pro-Trump people, as well as how reputable the outlets they worked for were. When I say that my anxiety drives me to crazy levels, I mean it. This is how I have always approached anything I have ever been a part of, and though it usually causes the worst headaches and pains, I rarely regret the extra effort put in.

Immediately, I knew who I wanted to reach out to. Ironically, this was somebody who I had been introduced to through email about four years ago when a manager of mine had pitched her a story that she politely declined. I tried to phrase the email in a way that would convince her that my story would be one that would intrigue her readers. I knew I only had one chance at hooking this reporter and wanted to make sure I didn't have any regrets. She was a great journalist and somebody I trusted to put together an honest story, despite whatever views she may or may not have about my politics. Within eight minutes, she responded to me and wanted to talk.

I could tell that she wanted to write a very honest story describing my exact experience from getting onto the campaign and my experiences there to the fears I felt in my modeling career. She went into detail asking me about my experiences in the fashion world, and whether it was an agent, a photographer, or fellow model, I had a story for her. I can't even count the number of times that I was told how evil all Trump supporters are. Or how many times I walked into a photo shoot only to stumble right into a conversation on the likelihood of impeachment. Or the number of times that I had to listen to disgusting vulgar things being said about President Trump, his family, and his supporters. I had enough stories for a lifetime of articles and was excited to get even just a few them off of my chest for the first time. A few days later I awaited the reveal of my story in the *New York Post*.

To be perfectly honest, I was really scared—probably more nervous than I had ever been. These weren't like the nerves that I was used to from the ice, modeling, or anything else. I genuinely had no idea what was going to happen, if anything at all! I had basically thrown my modeling career out the window with this story; I knew nobody in the fashion world would work with me again. And though a part of me wanted this story to get buried and ignored and for everything to remain mostly the same, another part of me knew that with this, I would need to find some new goals and dreams as well as ideas for work, and I was petrified. Basically, I was all over the place (as usual). After the initial feelings of excitement that I had made this happen, especially by myself, had passed; the real feelings kicked in, and they weren't fun. It was a combination of fear and excitement, certainly a lot of nerves, and a tiny bit of regret that I convinced myself was all in my head. It was all in God's hands I told myself, as I closed my eyes on my last night as a secret Trump supporter.

I don't know what I was most afraid of in terms of people finding out. I knew how many people I had in my life who weren't going to leave my side no matter my politics—I could count them on the fingers on one hand. Everyone else was a toss-up. Funnily enough, my biggest concerns were my piercer and my skate sharpener. I'll explain. When I began skating again, I genuinely wanted to stop harming myself more than I even wanted to succeed in my comeback. Okay, that's a lie, I'd give an arm and a leg and anything else to be able to show the world what I can do on the ice again, but I really did want to stop. I knew that it had gotten more and more frequent and that the best thing I could do for my skating was to work on my mental health, so to stop cutting myself became my top priority. After a long lesson (which was usually more like a therapy session) with one of my coaches, he calmly asked me, "Do you remember each time that you hurt yourself?" I thought for a minute and then realized that I could in fact remember each time that I had sat alone on the floor of a bathroom, or closet, or lord knows where else, bawling my eyes out just wanting to feel some kind of pain that I was convinced I deserved. "Did you grow from each experience?"

"No," I thought, "not at all."

"Well, what if we change that?" he suggested. I was confused but ready for any and all advice that he or anyone could give me. After an hour or so of conversation with him and myself, I realized that when hurting myself, I didn't just want to inflict pain. My goal was actually to hurt myself to a point so painful that I would never make the same mistake again. Meaning that if there was a day when I destroyed my arm after a session where I didn't do the jump I wanted (my twenty-first birthday, for example), I was hoping that the pain I caused myself would be so serious that I would never miss the jump again. Basically, I hoped that I would fear myself so much, that I would learn from my mistakes and the self-inflicted punishment and never mess up the same way again. Unfortunately, as my coach pointed out that day, this had not worked nor helped me grow from each experience in any way. So I decided to try something new. I began getting a piercing every time I went through an experience that made me want to hurt myself. This way, I got to deal with a bit of pain, like my crazy self was convinced I deserved, and I was left with something beautiful to look at. The piercings also reminded me of the last time I wanted to, but did not, cut myself. It sounded crazy, but it worked for me. It gave me something special and meaningful to take with me everywhere I go, and more importantly, it made me stronger. I hope you know that I am very well aware of how crazy I sound. But it's important to me that anyone reading this understand the effects that giving your life to a sport can have on your well-being and mental health. And the effects that any mental health issues can have on the way we live our lives.

In fact, many things in life can lead us to mental health issues and I refuse to keep silent about mine, especially when I consider the possibility of helping even one person by speaking up. I've been through hell with injuries. My physical health right now, at just twenty-four years old, is actual shit. But when I was on crutches, in a cast, or even just had a visible scar to represent the pain that I was feeling, people understood. I did not have to pretend that I was doing alright because nobody would question the fact that I wasn't if they saw what my ankle looked like. But mental health is different. Not only do you constantly feel like you have to put on an act, but even when you find people you want to tell about your struggles, you almost always feel as though they will never under-stand the gravity of them because they cannot see them. You are constantly forced to try and prove that you are alright or just how sad you are in order for someone to take your problems seriously.

It is a really difficult and awful spot to be in, and one too many people around the world are suffering with right now.

Anyway, why am I telling you all of this? It's relevant, I swear! Luckily, I live in the greatest city in the world and am blessed to have some of the most interesting, intriguing, and special people all around me. And when I went looking for someone to trust with stabbing my ear with a needle, I found one of these very special people. Somehow, even in the combined few hours (in two years) that I had spent with this person, I had opened up to him more than most others in my life. I really don't think he expected to hear anything that he did when he casually asked, "What made you want another piercing?" But he not only took all of my stories extremely seriously, he made me feel like they were totally normal, which helped me more than he will ever know. Now Adrian is a serious lefty (the term he asked me to use to describe him), something I have zero issues with, but something that, of course, scared me when it came to him finding out my secret. Did I never want to trust anyone else with piercing my ears again? Sure, that was a part of it. But most of my concern was wrapped around the fact that I had so sincerely enjoyed his company and our conversations, I didn't want to lose him as a friend. He was someone I probably saw four times a year at most for a short visit and piercing, and yet that's what he was—a friend. Let me stress the fact that I don't have a lot of real friends, like basically zero. So, when there is someone whose conversation and presence I enjoy, they become extremely important to me. Adrian knew me, the real me, the me that so many wouldn't even believe existed once I became "that Trump girl." And I so badly wanted to keep people in my life who knew the real me. Losing him terrified me.

Another fear of mine was losing the guy who sharpens my skates. I know this sounds hilarious, and I am laughing as I write it, but there really are so few people in New York City that can sharpen figure skates properly—any figure skater here will vouch for this! Yes, he and I have less of a friendship, but I trust him once a month with my most prized possession. Genuinely, these were the people who crossed my mind and the concerns that rushed through my mind on that last night before my story was published for the world to see. Yes, it sounds funny, but these are real-life issues that so many deal with nowadays. The fact that I knew that I could lose these people in my life just because of who I voted for was already insane, even separated from the emotional connection that I may have had with them. And as I closed my eyes, it soothed my soul knowing that if anything, someone out there would feel less alone as they read my story and realized that so many out there share the same concerns.

Within a few hours of the story being released, I could no longer open my phone. The number of comments and messages, both kind and ridiculously cruel all at once, was incredibly overwhelming. One second, I was crying because somebody had called me a Nazi, and the next I was crying because somebody had told me that my story had inspired them to be braver themselves. I was a puddle of emotions as I realized just how incredibly cruel people could be at the same time that I realized just how scared so many others around the country felt, just like me. I watched as people I knew slowly began to unfollow me on Instagram, while others decided to do the same but only after first telling me how disgusting I was. Somebody that I grew up with decided to message me saying, "I always knew you were a racist." As if it made more sense to convince yourself that somebody who you knew and liked your entire life was a giant racist than to force yourself to wonder if maybe there was something that you were missing, if not about the president, at least about his supporters. I was much more overwhelmed than I thought I would be. And as prepared as I thought that I was to deal with the nasty comments, I was really surprised by the viciousness that so many people displayed toward me, a stranger.

I thought that the comments would eventually subside and that the story would blow over, but it certainly did not. A few hours after the story hit the news cycle, a producer from Fox & Friends reached out and asked me to be on the show the next day. Within twelve hours, I found myself vomiting backstage before my appearance on television on one of the most-watched programs in the United States—something I hadn't expected and something I had no idea how I would manage. After seeing my story in the *New York Post*, Lara Trump texted Darren to have him tell me that she was my biggest fan. It was a strange world that I had just entered into, and I had no idea how to feel about anything going on around me. A huge part of me wanted to cancel and disappear. All I could think about was how much I wanted to go back into hiding, but it was too late. There were Americans from all across the country telling me that I was inspiring them and Americans from all across the country trying to silence me. In the moment, all I could wonder was why such attention was being thrown my way when I hadn't done anything of any real significance. My entire life, all I had dreamed of was for the world to see me skate. And here I was, receiving an insane amount of attention for something that could not be further from that dream. I had to make a choice in that moment. I thought to myself, what would twelve-year-old Elizabeth do?

And I headed to the set.

15

In the month that followed my announcement, I got to tell my story practically everywhere. By "everywhere," of course, I mean the news outlets that would have me on. So, from Fox, to The Daily Wire, to Breitbart, and anywhere else that you can think of, I was there. Not surprisingly, nobody from the more liberal media wanted to have me on their shows or outlets. To be quite honest, I was incredibly anxious all the time at that point, so it was helpful to be able to tell myself that the people I was speaking to would be friendly. However, I knew I had a message for people, and I knew those who needed to hear it were not all watching Fox News. I desperately wanted to show people my side of things in the hopes of bringing people together. Unfortunately, I very quickly learned that it would not be that simple.

I received, and I'm not exaggerating, thousands of messages. Some people were too nice for words, and others were astonishingly unkind. My emotions were bouncing up and down by the minute, but I still wasn't used to it. No matter how many messages

I read, both kind and cruel, each one still shocked me just as much as the last. I actually think it was the cruelty that surprised me more than anything. People had absolutely no problem at all saying some of the most despicable things that I had ever heard to a perfect stranger. It wasn't even the cruelty of the comments that upset me as much as the realization that there were this many people in the world, and in our country, who felt perfectly okay hurting somebody they didn't know. I've always had my fair share of issues with the beliefs on the political left. Not even with the left, maybe, as I hate labels, but with certain topics and issues that I happen to feel very, very strongly about. Does that mean that I would ever even consider sending a message to someone in the hopes of hurting them? Of course not. It sickened me to think of the people, on both sides of the aisle, who had been doing this to others. It also hurt to think of those who had been affected by it. People often forget just how hurtful words can be, no matter where or who they come from.

I worried so much before coming out with my secret that my mind might eventually change. I didn't think I would stop supporting President Trump, however, I did worry that I might have some kind of epiphany about everything that I was sharing with the world. Maybe that the bullying was for some reason warranted? Or simply that I didn't think there was a big enough issue for me to deserve any stories in the first place. Fortunately, or maybe unfortunately, that is not at all what happened. I very quickly discovered just how many people out there were struggling with exactly what I had been feeling, and on both sides of the political aisle. I learned through the messages I was receiving, from the conversations I was having, and from the comments and interactions between others that I was seeing, that so many others around the country felt judged and attacked for their views—something that should never, ever be happening in the United States of America. I know I've said that quite a few times at this point, but I really cannot stress to you how shocked I was by the level of viciousness between people, simply over political views. I had assumed that I went through some rough stuff because I was in New York City or part of the modeling world. But it turned out that that had nothing to do with it. People were evil to each other everywhere. It was simply dreadful to see.

My parents and grandparents fought to come here specifically because of this reason. They wanted to make sure that the lives of their future children and grandchildren would never have to be like theirs and that they and everyone around them would get the opportunity to think, feel, speak, and vote freely and without attacks. Everything I was seeing broke my heart. People were telling me that they were scared to tell their coworkers, friends, and even parents about their views. People on the right and the left were dealing with this all across the country, for the first time in quite some time in our country's history, and it was something I knew could not continue. I realized that my message was so much clearer and so much bigger than I had originally thought, and I very quickly gained more confidence in myself, my words, and my message.

It was extremely difficult for me to feel the hatred all around me. Some days it felt like the entire world was against me. But unfortunately, that was not even the worst part. It was when people who I had known for years, or had even grown up with, began to turn on me that my heart broke. Telling me that they didn't appreciate my views would have been completely fine. Even ending our friendships would have been fine with me, if it was something that they felt they needed to do. But to call me racist, sexist, or homophobic all because of who I voted for was completely baffling to me. We had gone years, even decades in some occasions, being friends, so how come they were just now deciding that I must be one of these terrible things? I always believed that actions meant a hell of a lot more than words, and I tried to live my life committed to that. For all of these people who I had loved and trusted, to throw away all of my actions and call me one of these disgusting things was completely inexplicable to me. I thought that I had proven myself to them over the years, and yet they had no problem tossing that all away and accusing me of being a totally dreadful person.

All I wanted to do was prove myself. I felt like I needed the entire world to know that I was not the completely evil person that everybody was accusing me of being. And yet, I learned pretty quickly that that is exactly the opposite of what our lives should be about. Even if there was a magical way to convince the entire world to love you (which there isn't), it would take your entire lifetime, if not longer. That is no way to live your life. I realized almost immediately that my life was going to change. I had always wanted people to like me. I was incredibly sensitive, even as a little girl, and wanted everybody to know that I was a good person. For some reason, the idea of people having negative opinions about me always floated in the back of my mind, no matter what I was doing. It was something that had consumed my life, especially on the ice, and something I had always accepted as a part of my anxious personality. But I learned that people's opinions really do not matter, mostly because you just can't let them. I try to be nice to everybody, no matter what. As long as I do that, and as long as I realize that I answer to nobody except God, there is nothing and nobody left for me to worry about. You will never, ever convince the world to love you; all you can do is make sure to treat everybody with respect as you continue to fight for your own beliefs, while realizing that they may never be liked or accepted by anybody around you.

And as great as this was a lesson for me to learn, it didn't solve all of my problems. I knew that, despite it being difficult, I was learning an incredibly valuable lesson—one I wish I had learned a very long time ago and one that would have saved me a lot of hardship over the years. However, it didn't help me when facing the dark reality that my life was never going to be the same again. Something I really didn't see coming was the idea that the rink could become an even more uncomfortable place than it already was. My anxiety was always at its worst when I was at the rink, trying desperately to distract myself from my own negative thoughts about my success, focusing on breathing through the physical pain of skating, and having to constantly think about avoiding certain people. To put it bluntly, despite my love for skating, the rink was not a fun place to be for me, and telling my Trump campaign story publicly only made it that much worse.

People who regularly said hi to me began to completely avoid even looking in my direction. It was as if they didn't want to seem as though they were friendly with the "Trump girl," as I often heard myself being described. It brought even more discomfort to an already unpleasant situation, and one I genuinely didn't even consider could get much worse. A few days later, my choreographer decided that he would no longer work with me. I had known him for years, assuming like I wrongly did with others, that he would not change his opinion of me just because of my support for the president.

He had finished about 75 percent of the programs that we had been working on. We had worked for quite some time on my short and long programs, so that I could have them ready to compete when I (hopefully) was able to make my comeback. So not only was his work never going to be performed, but I had to start over completely, trying to avoid thinking about how much money was wasted. Worst of all, I'm simply going to miss him. As you can clearly tell, skating has been incredibly personal for me with all that I have been through. And being around his overwhelming talent made me feel so good about returning to a sport that I missed so much. Missing him has actually been more difficult than some of the friends that I lost, probably because I hadn't even realized how much he meant to me.

Ready for the most ironic part? He already knew that I supported the president. My coach told him back in 2017 after I had finished my work on the campaign and let the secret slide to the few people that I trusted. I'm sure he didn't like that part of me, but he knew it, and he still worked with me. He also continued to share personal things with me. In a way, maybe because of us being closer in age, I had considered him even more of a friend than a coach. But why did he suddenly decide he could no longer work with me? Because one of his students is well known, specifically

Elizabeth Pipko

for his anti-Trumpness, and would not accept it if he worked with me, I'm sure. Somehow that made it even worse. Would I have been upset if he had chosen on his own to stop working with me? One hundred percent, but I would have understood. However, we had a relationship. Not a romantic one, maybe not even an overly friendly one, but one that meant a lot to me, and that was now gone.

Of course, with all of this going on at once, I was also trying, unsuccessfully, to avoid the crap being written about me on the internet. And though there were so many lies about my education, marriage, modeling career, and my family, the ones that hurt the most were the ones about my skating. I can spend my life proving these people wrong when it comes to my education, or career, or even my marriage (though I shouldn't). But unless I actually get my butt back on the ice and perform at the level I once did, I can't prove anybody wrong when it comes to what they said about my skating. People will never know, not only how much this sport means to me, but that I was once good at it. I always thought that I had a huge future in the sport and have gone through hell and back trying to accept everything that happened and to be okay again. And just as I was slowly beginning to forgive myself and to accept where I was, some hateful people thought that they should tear me down because they hate the person in the Oval Office. How fair is that? There is even a personal essay that I once published online detailing my injury and everything that I was going through when first trying to come back—from the injuries, to the panic attacks, to the sexual harassment—and if they had searched my name for just two minutes, they most likely would have seen it and known my story. But they didn't want to. They wanted to tear me down, so that it appeared as if every one of the president's allies was a liar and a fake. As if because I voted for him, I deserve to have every part of my life and mental health torn apart. Because in the 0.0001 percent chance that that could hurt the president, it was worth what it did to me.

This is what most of the media cares about right now, above anything else. They care about tearing down the president and anybody who he knows, no matter the cost. They don't seem to care who they hurt in the process or wonder if what they are doing is right. This is what journalism and news has become. And not only is it unfortunate because these people do not realize who they could be hurting, it is unfortunate because it can change our entire country as a whole. And yes, I'm talking about the liberal-leaning mainstream media, because that is where I have felt this from. But yes, I will gladly say that I know that this comes from both sides of the media, however with Trump becoming the president and more of the media being left-leaning, you can probably see where I'm coming from when I say a lot of it right now is aimed from one side.

People around the world, especially young people, need others to look up to. I've said it before and I'll say it again, my parents taught me when I was very young that there was something to learn from everybody, no matter who they were or whether our views aligned or not. This is something I have always believed in. But now, to know that so many people who are looked up to are only focused on hurting people they do not know in the hopes that it brings down Donald Trump, it feels like the foundation of our country is being torn apart. It's something that was, thankfully, never allowed under Obama's or Bush's presidencies, or anyone's before that. But suddenly, in 2016, people began feeling alright with hurting others as long as they were in any way connected to President Trump—something extremely dangerous for all involved and something I hope to fight against no matter what it takes.

Before 2016, people judged others not by their political affiliations, but by their intentions. I remember listening to my parents' political disagreements with their friends and always being very aware of the lack of tension in the room. This was because nobody questioned the other's intentions. They may have disagreed politically about the best policy decisions for the future of our country, but the underlying truth was that both sides wanted the best for the United States of America. It was easy to debate when people appreciated each other's opinions, even when disagreeing. Nobody ever insulted the other or assumed terrible things about them just because they had a different approach to reaching the same goal. It was the reason that I fell in love with politics at such a young age. I watched people who came from totally different backgrounds and believed completely opposite things come together with one goal: a better tomorrow for future generations. That was all politics was, and I freakin' loved it. And somehow, here we are today, instead using politics as an excuse to judge and slur our coworkers, peers, friends, and family.

I was still hopeful. America has and always will be the greatest country in the world. And despite the attacks from strangers and friends, I knew that there were good people out there. I just had to stay strong until I found them, and maybe even more importantly, inspire others to do the same. I was upset with so many who had disappointed me with their words and actions, but at the same time, I had hundreds, if not thousands, of people telling me that they would be there for me, and it was extremely reassuring. Speaking of, if anyone reading this right now messaged me at any point, thank you! I hope that I got back to you, but if I didn't, I'm sorry and it's really important to me that you know that your message had a little part in helping me be okay with everything going on around me.

Remember Adrian? The man responsible for piercing holes into my ears who I was so afraid of losing? Well, after a long night of reading nasty articles about myself (I've stopped doing this, I promise), I checked my phone and found a text message from him. I'm going to share a part of it here in the hopes that it inspires you as much as it inspired me that night.

"I feel like we get so caught up in the 'this side vs that side' mentality that we forget that we are all people with different thoughts and opinions on how we get to the common goal; and that's life, liberty, and the pursuit of happiness for everyone. So, I'm sure you're getting a lot of heat right now from people who aren't Trump supporters. But if it means anything, I'm not one of those people that sees you any differently from when I first met you. I hope you feel a good pressure off your shoulders and know that even though we don't agree, you have a friend in me."

That message is the reason that I love and believe in America as much as I do. Adrian and I could not be more different, and at a time when he could have easily blocked my number, he chose to do something nice. He chose to not only accept me for my beliefs, but to take the effort to send me a message of support, making sure that I knew I still had a friend out there. People like Adrian are the reason I keep fighting; people like him are the reason we must all keep fighting. Because what we have right now, what we have allowed ourselves to become—that is not the United States of America that I want to be a part of. More importantly, it is not the United States of America that my parents, my grandparents, and so many others have fought to be a part of.

Adrian will probably never know what his text that day meant for me. But I get to take his words with me wherever I go and whenever I need to remind myself of all the good people out there in the world. There have been days where people were so nasty to me that all I wanted to do was to be nasty right back and walk away from all of this. But I didn't, because I want to be like Adrian. Kindness will always be more powerful than anger, especially anger that stems from politics. Don't get me wrong, there are policies that I really care about. But I know what's most important in life, and that's kindness and empathy for others. In fact, the best way to try and get others to begin to understand the policies that you believe in is probably with kindness.

So next time you meet someone who you disagree with, choose kindness, and choose to be like Adrian. You never know what it might mean to someone.

16

I still had no idea what I was doing in life, but I was being brave, something I hadn't done in years, and it felt pretty good. I knew that I had to do something with the tiny platform that I now had, but I had no idea what. The one thing I did know was that I was probably going to be stuck in politics for some time as nobody outside of that world would want to hire an outspoken Trump supporter. I began to brainstorm, but while dealing with all of the chaos that was now around me, I quickly realized that in order to stay in politics, I would need to do something that was important to me. It would need to be something worth fighting for, no matter the attacks that I knew would only get worse if I stayed in this world. My parents had always told me that no matter what stage I was at in my lifetime, a person needed an anchor. And whether that was my family, God, or Judaism in general, there was always something that kept me grounded and away from bad choices or extra confusion. This was what I was going to need to find if I wanted to continue on in the brutal political world. I sat up many nights thinking about all that I had done to my life. I wondered where I was going next and tried to come up with something that would make those around me proud. I often found myself thinking about my grandfathers looking down on me and everything I was dealing with and wondering what they would want me to do, wishing that I could have just thirty seconds with any of them to get the advice I so desperately needed.

I've spoken about three of my grandfathers but have not yet mentioned the fourth. Yes, I was extremely lucky and had four grandfathers looking out for me and loving me like only a grand-father can. My step-grandfather, who despite not being related by blood, loved my brother and me as if we were his own, was a Romanian Jew and a Holocaust survivor, as well as a lifelong Democrat. A lot of my childhood was actually spent asking my parents who the Clintons were because I had heard him talk about them so often and so affectionately. Unfortunately, he was diag-nosed with cancer in early 2016 and, by the spring of 2016, only had a few weeks to live. We rarely spoke about politics because I knew where he stood, and again, before 2016, there was so much more to most people's relationships than Donald Trump and Hillary Clinton.

While in hospice care one night, he was laying in his bed and flipping through the television channels, when he stopped on one of the news networks that was playing one of then-candidate Donald Trump's speeches.

He turned to us and said, "Promise me you will vote for Donald Trump."

He passed away a week later.

I had always wanted to ask him what it was about Trump that made him want to support him. He was a proud Democrat and a proud American. But before anything, he was a proud and devoted Jew. I knew how much it must have meant to him to even consider wanting to elect a Republican president, and I knew that there could have been no reason stronger for his decision than his faith. I wondered what there was that I could do that I knew would make all four of my grandfathers proud of me. My brother-in-law had sent me a message right after my grandfather passed away in 2017 and told me that the most important thing I could now do with my future, and in his honor, was to live a life that would make him proud. He was exactly right.

I set out to meet with the few Republican Jews who I had known about and admired, hoping that I would meet someone who could inspire me with an idea for my future. I knew some of the things that I was interested in and hoped that I would find somebody who could help to put me on the right path and who could act as a mentor, something I knew I would need in the tough world of politics. But as I have said probably too many times already in this book, "man makes plans and God laughs." Within maybe three weeks, I was announced as the spokesperson for "Jexodus," a slogan meant to represent the "Jewish exit" from the Democratic party. Within just a few days, I found myself back on Fox & Friends, luckily not vomiting backstage this time, and cautiously sharing my thoughts on how the right is a far better and more supportive place for American Jews than the left is today. All of a sudden, the attacks on me got a lot worse. Some days, I would wake up scared to open my phone. There were a few days where I couldn't open my computer or go on the internet because of the amount of negative and even false stories being written about me. I think the few weeks following my Fox & Friends appearance were some of the hardest of my life. Between the things being said about me all over the place, and the anxiety and overthinking that fills my brain even on regular days, it felt like the entire world was out to get me.

Was I shocked at the world's reaction to what I was doing? Not this time. I once heard the saying, "nobody hunts small deer," and that's exactly what I was about to learn. Just like when I had been bullied by friends and family members when I first began skating, it seemed like everybody wanted to bring me down, just for pushing an idea that was different. I had taken on the Jewish vote, something that many in politics have relied on and taken for granted for years, and that made people afraid and uncomfortable.

I don't think they were scared of anything specifically. I certainly don't think I posed much of a threat to anyone, at least not at that point. But I was messing with something that nobody had dared to touch for years. "Jews always vote Democrat," I was told during what felt like every political conversation I had ever had, as if that were a reason to stop trying to inform Jewish Americans of what both parties are doing in terms of their interests. Or to stop taking the Jewish vote for granted, something that the left has done for decades now and something very common on both sides of the aisle when it comes to those who don't happen to be swing voters. As an American Jew, I felt like the values that I was raised on were not being heard or acknowledged, and I wanted to start a movement to change that. Politicians in general tend to favor the voters that they desperately need to swing over to their side to win an election, or the voters that they know will send money their way—that's it. It's a dirty game, but that's the game of politics, and it absolutely happens on both sides of the aisle. Which is why I thought this needed to be done. This wasn't political for me. This was about my faith and what I genuinely thought was best for the Jewish people. Again, something I could never fault someone else for doing, even if I didn't agree with their political beliefs.

All I wanted to do was to open people's minds to the idea that there may be another choice. I care about my fellow Jews in a way that will never compare to any political beliefs I have. The

Jewish people have been through so much and there really are so few of us; I do consider each and every one of us connected in one way or another. And whether you agree with me politically or not, I genuinely thought it would be understood by fellow Jews that everything I was doing was out of the goodness of my heart. Clearly, I was extremely naïve and extremely wrong. I was attacked for absolutely everything, and mostly by fellow Jews. I was sick to my stomach every single morning, terrified of what I would see when I opened my phone, genuinely not thinking I would be able to continue on with what I was doing. Like most of us have unfortunately had to learn during our lives, when the attacks come from people you don't expect, that's when they hurt the most. And guess what didn't help at all with the negative attention? The president of the Unites States of America tweeting about me.

If they didn't hate me before, they all certainly did now! I very quickly found myself crying myself to sleep again. The anxiety disorder I had been diagnosed with years ago when I first attempted to skate after my injury reared its head again. Eventually, I was diagnosed with a bad stomach ulcer that kept me off of my feet completely for almost three weeks. I had literally stressed myself out to the point of an ulcer forming inside of me, leaving me unable to stand up or eat for weeks. But I didn't stop; I couldn't. Because that's exactly what they would have wanted, and you can never give your haters what they want. I had based my entire life around doing things that others tried to stop me from doing. There was no point in changing my personality now. All I wanted to do was to channel the twelve-year-old Elizabeth that I once was in order to take on all the hate that was being thrown my way.

Sadly, the most painful hate again came from those closest to me. And it pains me so much to write this, but I know that I have to. I never believed my dad growing up when he told me how many people out there would want the worst for me, but he was absolutely right. I don't consider myself special or successful. I don't consider anything that I've done to be noble or astonishing. And yet the second that I was an inch closer to fame or success than I had been before, the attacks began. When *The Forward* published a hit piece on me, I fell apart. I don't want to say it because it makes me sound weak, but it's the truth. That was the piece that attacked my skating more than any other, and it completely broke me. They claimed that they knew for sure that everything about my skating career had been made up. The attacks on every other part of my life were obvious lies, but none hurt like the ones about my skating. It's the one thing I feel like I have given absolutely everything to, the one thing that has caused me to have to go through so many obstacles and setbacks, and the one thing I thought would be off limits and respected by journalists who could so easily find something else about me to attack in their hopes of bringing down any voter of Trump's. I was heartbroken after reading it. All of my fears and sadness around skating come not just from the fact that it was taken away from me by injuries, but the idea that I know I may never get to share my skating with the world, which only leaves my skating memories to hold on to. And they destroyed those memories publicly, causing me to have one of the worst breakdowns I've had in quite some time. And the cherry on top of the whole situation? I found out a few weeks later that members of my own family took that tabloid nonsense and showed it to my eighty-three-year-old grandmother in order to ruin our relationship. I was being torn apart online at a level like this for the first time in my life; I was opening my social media accounts only to receive death and rape threats. And at a time when I probably would've needed my family most, that's what they decided to do instead. Never in my wildest dreams could I have seen that coming.

I hate telling that story because it still tears me apart. My relationship with my family was now completely destroyed, something one would never think would be the repercussion of me simply forming a movement to try and fight anti-Semitism and encourage better policies for Jewish Americans and Israel. Why did I tell this story? For all of you. I want you to know, anyone reading this right now, that people will always try to hold you back, no matter what it is that you are trying to do. Sometimes that will come from people you never expected, people you thought would always be there for you, and that's okay. It's sad and it's awful, but it can never, ever stop you. No matter what career path you are on, the one thing that is always consistent is the level of hate that will grow for you the more successful you become. Jealousy is an extremely powerful and ugly emotion. It ruins relationships, friendships, and families daily. Don't ever let it bring you down. And remember, it only means that you're doing something right.

Eventually, everything calmed down—or maybe I just got used to it. I was now stuck as the face of a movement that I had never even planned on being a part of. Everything happened so quickly and in a way I still haven't understood. All that I knew was that I had to make sure that I did what was right. It felt like only a few hours had passed between the idea of "Jexodus" being explained to me and my appearance on Fox & Friends, speaking about it to the entire country. Everybody thought that this was some giant orchestrated operation, others accused it of being an "AstroTurf" campaign. But it was literally anything but. To this day, I have yet to discuss what went on behind the scenes, mostly because it hurt me and shocked me in a way that I was not prepared for; but it also gave me an amazing crash course on the evils and craziness in politics. "Jexodus" was a term, that's it. There was no organization behind it. There was no staff, no financial backing, no big names ready to promote the idea, nothing. It was a term that I did not come up with, but rather one that was presented to me, and a term that somehow dominated the internet almost instantly upon being said on television.

I trusted a few people who I certainly should not have trusted and ended up with what felt like the entire country suddenly looking at me for answers that I did not have. Sometimes I think it was a blessing. Maybe God wanted me exactly where I am now, and that was the only way to get there. Who knows? All I know is that I went from having no clue what I was going to pursue in politics to being the spokesperson of a movement that everybody assumed was a big organization when, in fact, it was nothing. In what felt like years, but was actually only about five weeks, I quickly learned that what my dad had told me was correct: you can't trust anyone except yourself.

I take very few things seriously. In fact, everyone who knows me knows that about 95 percent of the conversations I have are sarcastic. I take a few things seriously in my life: my family, my country, my religion, and my skating. That's basically it. And the "Jexodus" situation was messing with too many of those things for me to take it anything but seriously. I immediately got to work on what I knew had to be the most well thought-out strategy for the future of the movement. I've said it before, and I will say it again, I do not believe in half-assing anything, and certainly not something on this scale. Nothing I have ever done in my life came easily or through "luck," as others often like to think. It was always hard work and the discipline that only a set of Russian parents can drill into you at a young age.

My entire life, I have known that if I wanted something done, I would have to do it myself, and if I wanted to succeed at whatever I was doing, I would have to work harder than I ever had before. It's something I often warn others about, though they usually choose not to listen, just like I did when my parents first told the same to me. I learned, when I was just getting on the ice at ten years old, that if I wanted to prove to anyone that they should take me and my dreams seriously, I would have to spend the time normally spent with a coach by myself, mastering the moves that I would need to impress others. As a teenager, I learned that even though doctors will tell you they want to help, when it comes to recovering from an injury in order to pursue your dream, you're unfortunately going to be left on your own with nothing but the YouTube videos you can find showing proper rehabilitation exercises. During my recovery, I found the dream coach that I had wanted to work with if my ankle ever healed; he was the former Chinese Olympic team coach, and I knew that in order to study with him I would need to know basic Chinese. So, in high school I took an extra class and studied honors Chinese for three years.

When Wilhelmina Models kicked me out of their agency, did I cry and mope? Yes, for a day. And then I pretended to be my own agent and got myself more work than they ever got me, eventually helping me sign with DAS models, the agency that I wanted to work with next. I think you're getting the idea.

And so, when I got stuck with no plan or future for this movement that I had been thrust to the forefront of, I knew that I needed to get to work. I knew how much this movement meant not just to me, but to so many others. And so, with the help of some amazing people, and a few months of very hard work, I launched The Exodus Movement. What started with a tweet and a few ideas eventually turned into a nonprofit, and then a super PAC. I was never going to be the person who felt comfortable taking people's money and leading a movement with no measurable results (something I eventually learned is how most people in politics spend their time). This was too meaningful and too important, and I was always going to treat it as such.

17

I'm not going to get into the details of everything that came before the forming of The Exodus Movement, mostly because it's quite boring. All I will tell you is that politics is not what it seems to be. In fact, the world is not what it seems to be. I grew up with a dream of working in politics one day. Before I discovered skating, I was a little girl obsessed with George Bush and Hillary Clinton and everybody that I was seeing on TV. All I wanted was to be a part of American history and to do what I could to make the world a better place. It may seem a little idealistic, but that's exactly what I was. I wanted to make people's lives better, and I wanted to make important decisions, because I was twelve and that's exactly what I thought politics was. In fact, that is kind of what I believed politics was until very recently. But boy, did I get a wake-up call. I hate to be the one to say it. And more than that, I hate that others much more experienced than me aren't saying it themselves. Which is why I will: politics sucks. Since getting involved in the political world, I can honestly say that I have met some of the worst human beings I hope to ever meet. Every single day, I am shocked by somebody's behavior. And this, by the way, applies to both the right and the left. I have met some of the biggest egotistical maniacs that I genuinely thought only existed in movies. Some days I can't believe these people exist at all, let alone in a field that I am somewhat a part of.

The hypocrisy that surrounds me constantly is the thing that I am most excited to get the hell away from one day. It's what the television shows and movies have been warning us about for years and years, and yet we have not caught on. Ninety-nine percent of people in the political world are hypocrites. They say the things they know they need to say in order to win a vote, or to pass a law, or to help somebody else do one of the two. And that somebody else that they're helping, they're not helping them because they like them or trust them for the job. No, they're helping them because they have a big "R" or "D" next to their names. Politicians are just propped-up robots trying to do their best at representing the interests of all the donors who are backing them while lying to the smaller donors without getting caught. It's a sick, sick world, and the fact that everybody knows that and still treats it like anything but is the sickest part.

These are the same people who go after each other for supporting policies that they once supported themselves. But because it is no longer helpful for them to support those policies, they decide to change their vote and to attack those who don't—despite being on the same side what feels like just yesterday. These are people who want what's best just for those around them and nobody else, hoping that they can manipulate the media to make sure that nobody catches on. These are people who are literally sitting on television and calling out corruption or sexual abuse while facing or covering up allegations of the exact same things themselves. These are people who know that their status as a politician and connections will get them through life without any bit of genuine thought, emotion, or compassion. I've been in politics less than two years, and I've already seen so much dirty, disgusting behavior that it keeps me up at night. Anybody who is able to witness this kind of thing for decades and continue pretending that they are confident that those around them are not participating in this type of behavior is lying, end of story. I can go on and on, but I think you get the point.

In order to succeed in politics, it seems like you have to sell your soul to the highest bidder and to continue letting people pass it around until the day you die. Yes, that was slightly morbid, but that's what I've learned. And it was crushing to me at first, mostly because no matter how much Darren warned me, I simply refused to believe him. He told me on several occasions that politics was going to be a nightmare for anybody who wants to do good more than they want power and fame. So, I guess the good news is, I have learned that no matter how badly I may want to or need to, I couldn't sell my soul—no matter how much anyone gave me for it. But the bad news is that I'm constantly surrounded by those who sold theirs a long time ago.

No matter how many of them there are and how powerful they think they are, no politician can or should ever matter to you more than those you love. That's something I want everyone to remember. Politicians are always answering to someone. The amount of dirt that is behind every candidate, politician, and political operative is so overwhelming, it will simply never be all about the people for any of them. That's another reason I supported President Trump. You can disagree with me on the effectiveness and goals of his policies, but it genuinely was a breath of fresh air (especially after everything I know now) to know that our president could be someone who wasn't a career politician and someone who didn't literally belong to thousands of people and groups around the world.

I don't believe that any person's vote should be taken for granted. And I genuinely believe that the Democratic Party abandoned the Jewish people long ago, while assuming that they could just simply go on counting on their votes forever. As if Jewish Americans, or any Americans for that matter, are too stupid to check someone's record or views before voting for them or to check the facts that they know are not being properly reported.

There have been plenty of times that both sides have said and done things that Jewish Americans should be worried about; nobody is trying to dispute that. However, living in the past can do absolutely nothing except keep us away from our future. And I refuse to let anybody I care about live so deeply in the past that they completely turn a blind eye to all that is happening right now. Look, we have the best president for Jewish Americans and for the United States–Israel relationship that we have ever had. I'm not asking you to like Donald Trump. In fact, I'm not even asking you to consider voting for him. All I'm asking of you is to admit to yourself the good that he has done for Israel. I think that's an easy place to start, and an important one. Ninety-five percent of Jewish Americans admit to supporting Israel and its right to exist. So why am I being called a Nazi by fellow Jews for supporting a president who has done all that he can do to keep Israel safe? Let's start there.

These are the conversations that I hope to be able to have and encourage so that we can start healing our country. These are the things that we need to focus on in order to stop the divide in our country that feels as though it is only growing wider by the day. There are a lot of issues that I feel passionate about—some that lean right and others that lean left—and yet I have just as hard a time debating either one of them when I am speaking with someone who disagrees with me. I genuinely think the mainstream media is against our president and his supporters to a point that is dirty and unfair. I don't think that because I've seen it discussed on Fox News or on the president's Twitter. I say that because I have lived it and felt it. However, that doesn't mean that we as people must stoop to the same level and treat others who we disagree with as if they are our enemies.

I think that abortion is a topic where I see the hatred and poisonous behavior between both sides really get worse by the day. It's one of the things I am most passionate about, and the reason that I considered myself a conservative at a young age. I knew absolutely nothing about politics but had learned about abortion and decided that if conservatives were pro-life, then I must be a conservative. It's one of the only opinions that I have stuck to for years despite being called every name in the book as early as middle school. There have been many policies that I thought I had made up my mind about. But, of course, my parents were right in telling me to calm down and take the time to learn from others before I just decided that I knew what I believed in and agreed with. Abortion has been one of the only things that hasn't changed in my mind. I am pro-life, and I'm extremely proud of that. That doesn't mean I don't have some issues with many in the pro-life movement who think it is appropriate to push their views on victims of incest or rape. It just means that I am pro-life, but also rational and open-minded and happy to listen to those around me that are pro-choice. It also means that I don't call those who are pro-choice "murderers" or "baby killers," because I know that it will not help solve any problem. And I ask and encourage those who are pro-choice to try and do the same as well. The idea that claiming that one side is evil could change anyone's minds is ridiculous. And in the end, all it has done is created a larger divide, especially among women, who should be standing together in difficult times and decisions, not far apart. I choose to proudly be pro-life, but to do that while also remembering that those who are pro-choice genuinely think that is best and do not understand where I am coming from.

Everything that I said about those politicians, by the way, no longer applies to just them. It used to be that just the politicians were corrupt. Then, suddenly, it became more and more people simply involved in politics. Recently we have seen the media turn itself upside down into an anti-Trump machine. Why? Because we have allowed them to. We have allowed these powerful and connected people to play us against each other for their own gain. We have allowed people to use the election of Donald Trump to try and reverse all of the good in the United States of America. And it is up to us, and only us, to try and turn everything back to normal. Those at the top do not care. They never have and they never will. Do you know why? Because they don't have to. Nothing will ever happen to their lives if they continue on as they have. It's us, normal people, who have let the media and the politicians turn Jews against Jews, teachers against students, and parents against children, and for what? What have we done to ourselves? What have we become? And at what cost?

Being a Jew means everything to me. It is something that always has and always will come before politics. I was raised on the idea of "Jewish solidarity," the notion that no matter where we are, we can find fellow Jews and feel as though we are with family. I was raised on stories of Jewish solidarity, only to grow up and be called a Nazi every day by people across the country who don't like who I voted for. I hate it. Do you know what else I hate? That everything my parents and grandparents dreamed about when they came here is being torn apart in front of our very eyes because people are upset about the results of an election. I hate everything about where we are right now, and I hope we can join together and put a stop to it immediately. Not for us, but for future generations who deserve to know the America that people all around the world dream about.

I want to share one more story because I think all people, not just Jews, should know the meaning of solidarity.

When my dad and grandmother left the Soviet Union, they took the train to Vienna. There, they were to be met by a representative of the Jewish agency in charge of helping Jews flee to Israel. Those who chose to flee to Israel would be flown immediately from Vienna; however, as they were now in a free country, they did not have to go to Israel but could choose to go anywhere. So my dad and grandmother chose to go to the United States. Neither of them spoke any Hebrew and felt as though the United States would be the better place for them. The head of this Jewish agency became so upset and erratic that he called them traitors to their own people. After they left Vienna and headed to Italy, the first stop on their way to the United States, the rules in the Soviet Union changed. Originally, you needed an invitation from a relative, any relative, from Israel to invite you to leave the Soviet Union and move there. However, the rules now said that the invitation had to come from a direct relative, meaning a parent or sibling. Because of this, my aunt was stuck in the Soviet Union, with no way to escape. So, what did my grandmother do? She called the man from the agency in Vienna, who had all but kicked them out of his office, and told him everything that was going on, explaining to him how desperate she was to save her daughter. And despite all of his original thoughts and feelings about the decision of my grandmother to come to the United States, a few weeks later he called her back and told her that he had found a man in Israel with the same last name, Pipko. He was a soldier in the Israeli army, so this agency had arranged for him to leave for a day in order for him to be able to go and make the arrangements for a visa invitation to be sent to my aunt back in the Soviet Union.

Nobody ever found out about what he had done, and notwithstanding the original disagreements or the fact that this man in Israel was a perfect stranger, they got my aunt out and probably saved her life, because of Jewish solidarity.

That is the kind of solidarity that we are missing today. Not just as Jews, but as Americans as well. There are men that have fought and died for us. There are soldiers currently fighting for us all across the world. And we can't sit at the same table with someone who has a different opinion on foreign policy? Really? And this is all because half of our country doesn't like the man in the Oval Office. It's absurd.

I have a lot of reasons for why I support President Donald Trump. But instead of trying to convince others of everything that I believe in, I've learned instead to try and find a middle ground. As I'm writing this right now, this is a list of a few things that President Trump has done in the past ten days:

- ✔ President Trump signed the Hong Kong Human Rights and Democracy Act.

- ✔ President Trump launched a federal initiative to address the crisis of missing and murdered Native American women, many of whose cases have gone unresolved for years.

- ✔ President Trump signed the Preventing Animal Cruelty and Torture Act, which will make intentional acts of cruelty to animals federal crimes.

- ✔ And President Trump surprised troops in Afghanistan with a visit on Thanksgiving.

I understand not voting for him. I even understand not liking him. But can we maybe agree that the above reasons are enough to understand why some others may support him? And that they do not deserve to be harassed, spit on, or attacked for it?

I just want us to go back to where we were before the 2016 election. I want people to go back to being kind to one another. And to go back to a time when they trusted their friends, family, and neighbors more than they trusted a political party.

18

Looking back on my life, I feel as though I have never fit in anywhere. That sounds like I'm complaining, but it's actually just the opposite. I have loved being myself, in every industry or group that I have ever been a part of. Sometimes not right away, but always by the end. From my day school to being homeschooled to being virtual schooled to my semester spent in the Professional Children's School, I remained me. And with every career choice that I have dipped my toes in since growing up, I have continued to do the same. Everything from modeling, writing, figure skating, politics, to the year I spent working for a restaurateur in his Michelin-starred restaurant (another dream of mine is to one day do something in the culinary industry), has made me what I am today. I have so many goals I have yet to even attempt to achieve, but I'm no longer worried, because I've learned the most important thing that I could ever need, and that's to go after each and every one of them, while staying true to myself. It all started as a little girl in school, realizing that I was going to be bullied for living life on my own terms, and it has continued on in every aspect of my life since then and brought me to where I am today, thanking God for those bullies and the path that their actions put me on. I've learned what it means to be an original, something I hope everybody reading this right now chooses to be. Remember, rules are meant to be broken. And if you don't break the rules, they will eventually break you.

When I started skating, nobody accepted me. First, I was shunned by my friends and family for wanting to skate in the first place, and later on, I was shunned by those in the skating world who didn't think I had a chance. Now, despite all of the physical obstacles that I have had to go through, it feels as though I won't ever have a chance of being regarded as a top skater. But who knows? Maybe I'm wrong and everything will change by the time I ever make it back to the sport I love more than life. And who knows? Maybe by the time that you're reading this, the world will have seen me skate again. Sometimes I wonder who I would be if I had never found skating, but I'll never know. Finding yourself isn't always about deciding where you want to go; instead, it's about seeing what to do with where you've somehow ended up.

You know what else I'm proud of? Getting to use the modeling world in order to turn into a more confident person but, at the same time, never letting it change me. The minute I walked into my first agency meeting at seventeen, I knew I didn't belong. It's a feeling I have gotten used to, and one I have actually learned to draw strength from today. Modeling was a real test for me. Learning how to take on a challenge like being a Wilhelmina model when I was at my lowest and saddest point was one that I am so proud that I embraced. But it certainly didn't come without its share of difficulties and confusion. Every time I met another model, I thought to myself, "where the hell am I?" I knew I didn't belong, but maybe that was the point. If I hadn't spent those years so completely out of my comfort zone, I probably wouldn't have had the courage and experience to be where I am today.

My religion has become a sensitive subject. Unfortunately, what used to be my favorite topic of discussion has become extremely sensitive due to everything going on around us. There is a rise in anti-Semitism, which only makes me want to flaunt my pride more than ever before. However, there is also a deep divide among Jews—not just in America, but in the world—because of the political climate surrounding us. I've been told I'm not a real Jew because of my politics. I've also been told by certain progressives that I focus too much on the religious aspect of Judaism and not enough on the cultural one. Ironically, I've also been told by many on the right that I am too involved in politics and culture and that I am not religious enough. In fact, every day another cyberbully decides to comment on my faith, always with another idea about what could be wrong with the way I choose to live my life. Many in the orthodox Jewish world do not understand me or why I choose to observe so many of the Jewish laws and customs, just like them, and yet take part in something like modeling swimwear. At the same time, reform Jews ask me why I waste my time following Jewish customs when they "clearly don't match my lifestyle," whatever that means. It's a confusing thing for many; funnily enough, that could probably be avoided if people just chose to let my relationship with God stay between Him and me.

Politics is the one place where I really thought that I was going to fit in. The Trump campaign was an adventure that I will always be grateful for, but did I find my place on that campaign? Certainly not. I found my voice and my strength and so many other things I so desperately needed at the time. But that doesn't mean that the experience didn't come with many feelings of confusion and discomfort that I hope to be able to explain properly one day. I learned a lot about myself on that campaign, mainly from others who taught me exactly what I did not want to become. Even after the campaign however, I was convinced that I was entering into a world with people as crazy and as driven as I was to make a change. I really thought that I had seen it all on our little 2016 campaign team and was ready for politics, but boy was I wrong! Politics is now my favorite world to be an outsider in. I feel like a complete outsider every single day, and with that, I draw the strength to make the decisions that I need to make for myself and those I love. Everyone I've met in politics has disappointed me. Some with their treatment of others, some with their insults and disrespect of me, some with their disrespect for the law, and so many others. It's been a whirlwind of crap, to be perfectly honest with you.

I've been incredibly lucky, and I know that. Which is why it's so hard for me to sit here and tell you how hard everything has been. 2019 was one of the most difficult years of my life. Just physically alone it was brutal. I got walking pneumonia in the beginning of the year, spent three weeks with a stomach ulcer unable to stand up in the spring, broke my hand in the summer, dislocated my knee twice in late summer, and spent almost three months between the hospital and my bed with pneumonia from October on. It was awful, but it doesn't compare to the crap that has come with being involved in politics. I know politics has changed since the 2016 election. In fact, most of what is going on now and much of what I have witnessed would not be happening at all if the 2016 election did not give us the results that it did. Donald Trump changed a lot of things, some for the worse and some for the better, and that's okay. The fact that I've had a front row seat to all of it has been such a blessing and a curse. It has taught me more than I could ever have learned anywhere else and given me two years that I probably could have otherwise only experienced in a movie theater.

I've also had to learn that it is most certainly a man's world. Some of the things I've witnessed men do and say have been so horrendous that it still hasn't registered as real life to me. I will never sit here and tell you that women have it as easy as men do, because that's simply not the case. I know what it has meant to try and do anything as a woman, and I certainly have had to face some things men couldn't even fathom. Then again, at least we know that it's a man's world, and that makes it easier to navigate and understand. I'll never stop standing up for women and the shit they have to go through to try and accomplish anything, specifically in the world of power and politics, because these past few years I've had a glimpse of that, and let me tell you, it isn't easy.

This last year in politics has also given me a gift I never thought I needed. For my entire life, I have been trying to prove myself. Since a very young age, I felt as though I needed to accomplish things in order for my life to be worth anything. Since getting injured, it has only gotten worse, with me trying to do even more in the hopes of making up for everything that I lost. I still have no idea where my skating can take me, but I know how much time I spent dealing with my injuries and how much I need to make up for. That is what used to consume my mind. And instead of modeling and politics helping to distract me and clear my mind of negative thoughts, it only added more pressure to my already over-anxious brain.

But since realizing that I really don't have much of a place in politics, I have calmed down a bit. No matter what I keep pushing myself to do, I am constantly learning that happiness cannot be measured by your accomplishments. I still have dreams and goals, don't you worry! And I plan to accomplish them all. But when you see something as ugly as the world of politics, it puts everything, even those dreams, into perspective. My husband always told me that no matter what I kept pushing myself to achieve in politics, I would always be unhappy, and I never believed him. Unfortunately, I'm someone so stubborn and hardheaded that I often need to make the mistake for myself, instead of listening to someone who already has.

Since being a part of a world as ugly as politics, I have begun to see everything in a much different light. There is beauty in the world at any second of the day, if you just choose to look for it. There is also ugliness in the world. Think long and hard about which one you want to spend your time around. I now enjoy my moments away from the computer and the nights where I can close my eyes and fall asleep peacefully without any negative thoughts or concerns. I enjoy dinners with my family more than I ever have before. Nowadays I even find myself stopping to pet more dogs, listen to more music, or take more photos with the people that I love. I spend more time working at the soup kitchen I loved volunteering in as a teenager, I spend more time learning about the things I'm curious about instead of the things I'm told I'm "supposed" to know, and I spend more time watching the movies and TV shows I like instead of forcing myself to keep up with the news. These are all new things for me, but they are gifts. Not only do I fear that I would have never discovered this part of the world if not for my experiences the past few months, but I fear that many others have yet to discover it as well.

Something else we often forget is that life is short and surrounding ourselves with those who matter to us is probably one of the most important things we can do. I lost a lot of friends when I came out with my secret of being a Trump supporter. But if I lost them for how I voted in an election, let's be honest, they were probably never my real friends. I've also met some pretty atrocious people in the last few months, making me cherish moments with my parents, husband, and brother that much more. My own relatives have turned on me quite disgustingly in the last few months. The things that they've said to me were things I could never imagine hearing from them just a year or two ago. But with success or attention of any kind, people's true colors come out— another reason that politicians probably should not be trusted. But the world is a big place, and there are some amazing people in it. So find them and make your life every bit as enjoyable as it can be. I promise just when you think you've seen it all, you'll discover even more magic than you ever even realized existed.

Though it's fitting with what I have written here, it is incredibly unfortunate what is going on in our world right now. If I haven't said it enough times in this book already, "man makes plans and God laughs." And though I hope God is not laughing right now, it is scary to think about how our entire world is changing as I write this. As I was looking over the final edit of this book, the world basically turned upside down. I sit here writing this right now as we deal with COVID-19 with no foreseeable end in sight. Everything that any of us had planned is now on hold, as we shift our gears to figuring out how to help those that need it. I'm praying for everyone affected by this virus and brainstorming how best I can help to pick up all the pieces when everything starts to come back together again. Who knows where any of us will be? All we can hope for is that we learn something from this and come back stronger and more united than we have ever been before.

We are all so lucky to be alive today in the single greatest country in the world. We are, hands down, the most decent country on planet Earth, and that is something that should be celebrated every single day. The last few years have not been easy, for anyone, but we ourselves created a lot of the tension that has taken over our country, and we ourselves can get rid of it. This is about a future for our children and grandchildren. A future filled with wonder, curiosity, kindness, strength, and free thinking—all the things that I am so privileged that I get to experience having been born and raised in the United States of America.

Remember "indivisible with liberty and justice for all?" Key word: *indivisible*.

Forty years ago, my grandparents had a dream: that one day, their legacy would get to continue on in the single greatest country in the entire world, led by the grandchildren they had yet to meet. Everybody in my family arrived in America with only ninety dollars in their pockets, and just one generation later, I ended up working on a winning presidential campaign. If that's not the American dream, I don't know what is.

My dad always likes to say that his American dream for us was different. When people think of the American dream, they think of capitalism and financial success. They think about making a life out of nothing, something you can only do in the United States of America and something that both of my parents have literally lived through. But my dad's dream for me was more than that. Did he want me to be successful? Of course. But more importantly, he wanted me to be me. In the Soviet Union everybody was raised to be a clone, with nobody having the liberty to pray, think, live, vote, or feel the way that they wanted to. That's why my parents and grandparents gave up everything they had—because no matter how hard you try, you can't put a price on freedom.

In the Soviet Union, you don't get to find your place. You're born into it. But in the United States of America, you can spend your entire life finding your place, no matter where that takes you. Because that's what it means to be an American; it means the ability to dream. I've experienced quite a few highs and lows in my life, but I wouldn't take anything back, because I get to spend every single day living my dream.

My American dream.

I've got a long road ahead of me when it comes to finishing the mission that my grandparents started, but I think I'm finally on the right track. They say not all those who wander are lost, and that's exactly right.

Do I know where I want to go?

Hell yeah.

I just need to figure out how to get there.

This book was published on August 25th, 2020,
forty years, to the day, since my father left the
Soviet Union.